'I highly recommend this b   r
and to learn how to pray s   l
Frank bring a wealth of expe   l
and humility to this topic f   :
power of prayer to bring abc
        Dr Lucy Peppiatt, Princi ...... *ιncological Centre, UK*

'This is a practical book on prayer which has clearly been written out of down-to-earth experience rather than ideas and theories. It acknowledges the link between passionate prayer and effective kingdom advancement. Prayer followed by action into our communities, together with unity and partnerships, becomes a recipe for greater levels of spiritual breakthrough.'

Stuart Bell, Senior Pastor, Alive Church and
Leader, Ground Level Network

'Some of the challenges facing society at present seem almost impossible to solve: drugs, gangs, knife crime and a society that has become more isolated and divided. The police are often the agency of last resort for many of these issues, but all too often we can only respond and fail to deal with the causes of the problems and simply can't provide the long-term solutions. However, working with organizations like Redeeming Our Communities across the country we can begin to make a difference. People of faith can begin to solve these social problems, and the power of prayer does make a difference even when faced with some of the most challenging situations. Francis of Assisi, when asked about dealing with what appeared an insurmountable problem, once said, "Start with what you can do, then do what's possible and you will soon find you are doing the impossible." People of faith taking action, backed by prayer, can transform our whole community.'

Paul Netherton, Deputy Chief Constable, Devon and Cornwall Police,
and President, Christian Police Association

'Few people I know have been as significant as Debra in terms of mobilizing and modelling prayer. I'm confident that this timely book will help many to realize afresh the vital need for the kind of movement of prayer that's been at the heart of every great move of God in our nation's history.'

Andy Hawthorne, CEO, The Message Trust

'Full of inspiring stories and a clear challenge to believe once more in the power of prayer. A must-read as we seek to see the UK transformed for Jesus.'

Gavin Calver, Director of Mission, Evangelical Alliance

'I have worked alongside ROC for many years, as well as Street Pastors and Street Angels, among others. Debra and ROC have shown the power of their approach and how prayer plays an integral part in harnessing shared purpose and endeavour within communities of greatest need. I work with police colleagues of many faiths and many of no faith – all are in awe when they witness what can be unlocked in this way and are humbled by the support they also receive from Debra and her wider network. Policing is full of people who choose their work because they are "purpose-driven" – and safer, kinder communities are what we all aspire to.'

Olivia Pinkney, QPM, MA, Chief Constable, Hampshire Constabulary

'There is a rising tide of prayer in our nation – and it can't go unanswered by God! For anyone who wants to be a part of it, as I do, here is great encouragement from someone who has prayed and seen mountains move.'

Paul Harcourt, National Leader, New Wine England

'As with everything Debra writes, says or does, *Mountain-Moving Prayer* is down to earth, practical, and with a strong biblical base for faithful, believing prayer. I know that when prayer is mentioned many Christians feel guilty or condemned. Read this book and allow Debra's experience to lead you into a fresh realization that you have a seat in the throne room of heaven and you are very welcome there.'

Ian Cole, World Prayer Centre

'Debra Green writes so fluently about faith because she has lived it all her Christian life. Certainly, she has a gift of faith which she has nurtured well, but beyond that she uses her gift to incite faith in others, around her own nation and beyond. That's how cities like hers experience drastic drops in crime, and strong economic growth, the restoration of families and the empowerment of ordinary people. Her insights into how faith can change our world are full of the integrity of a life that has proved these principles to be dynamically true. This is not a "painting-by-numbers" book, encouraging people rigidly to follow certain steps to success. No, this book holds life and light and hope with such enthusiasm and encouragement that the reader feels empowered to rise and follow Jesus, with greater awareness of his determination to transform us into agents of the kingdom, carrying the power to change our communities.

This book is fantastic. If you're serious about changing your world, or maybe just your street or workplace to begin with, this book will equip you. Get it for yourself, and buy more for your friends.'

Bev Murrill, speaker and author, and founder of Christian Growth International, Cherish Uganda, Liberti Magazine (UK), Kyria (UK and Australia) and Scarlet Women (Congo)

'If what stands in your way is too high to climb, too hard to dig or too big to go around – it's time for mountain-moving prayer!'

Anthony Delaney, Leader, Ivy Church and LAUNCH

'*Mountain-Moving Prayer* is a testament to what can be achieved through prayer. Starting from how individuals can grow their prayer life using the ingredient of faith, Debra shows how partnership in prayer can transform lives, communities and nations. Each chapter deals with one of the steps to building communion with God. It starts with baby steps from Base Camp and develops to the most powerful form of prayer, the prayer of agreement in prayer partnerships.

I would encourage everyone to get a copy of this book if they desire a vibrant prayer life and to have an impact on nations for Christ. It is a must read, relevant to every Christian no matter the level of their spiritual development. Debra has once again demonstrated the importance of prayer in the life of every believer and how, through prayer, we can capture the world for Christ.'

Abimbola Komolafe, Senior Pastor, Jubilee Church Manchester, Redeemed Christian Church of God

'It's been a privilege to observe Debra's faith journey over the past 20 years. She has lived what she writes. Her ability to hear God and push through in prayer despite the hurdles is inspiring. Who knows what else the Lord has in store on this remarkable journey?'

Canon Billy Kennedy, Pioneer Network Leader, New Community Church, Southampton, and President, Churches Together in England

'Debra has demonstrated in her life and work the impact of a truly intimate prayer walk with God. Her accomplishments are a testament to her skills and talents, but underneath all the great things she has accomplished have been the hidden and humbling roots of prayer. I'm sure many people will discover the strength to persevere by reading this book.'

Yinka Oyekan, The Gate Church, Reading

Debra Green, OBE, has become a key voice in the UK with respect to prayer and community engagement through her work with Redeeming Our Communities (ROC). After discovering key principles through her work in Greater Manchester, she has implanted the core ideas in many towns and cities across the UK. Her bestselling *City-Changing Prayer*, co-authored with Frank Green, has played a vital role in carrying the message to the wider Church.

Debra was awarded an OBE in 2012 for her work in the community. She is a well-established public speaker and is a member of the organizing committee for Spring Harvest.

Dave Roberts is a former editor of *Christianity* magazine. He is a co-author of prayer bestsellers *Red Moon Rising, The Grace Outpouring* and *The Way of Blessing*.

By Debra Green

CITY-CHANGING PRAYER: INSIGHTS FROM MANCHESTER'S
IMPACTING CITY-WIDE PRAYER MOVEMENT
(with Frank Green)

REDEEMING OUR COMMUNITIES: 21ST CENTURY
MIRACLES OF SOCIAL TRANSFORMATION

ROC YOUR WORLD: CHANGING COMMUNITIES FOR GOOD

MOUNTAIN
MOVING
PRAYER

THE UNLIMITED POTENTIAL

DEBRA GREEN OBE
WITH DAVE ROBERTS

First published in Great Britain in 2019

Society for Promoting Christian Knowledge
36 Causton Street
London SW1P 4ST
www.spck.org.uk

British Library Cataloguing-in-Publication Data
A catalogue record for this book is available from the British Library

ISBN 978-0-281-08137-0
eBook ISBN 978-0-281-08138-7

1 3 5 7 9 10 8 6 4 2

Typeset by Falcon Oast Graphic Art Ltd.
Printed and bound by CPI Group (UK) Ltd, Coydon, CR0 4YY

eBook by Falcon Oast Graphic Art Ltd.

Produced on paper from sustainable forests

For Frank.
Your love and support has made it all possible.

Contents

Acknowledgements

Our thanks to everyone who has sent us such kind endorsements for this book. Your words have truly encouraged us.

Special thanks go to Frank Green who has a really good eye for editing and has helped us refine and polish each chapter.

We are grateful to many friends who have shared their prayer journey with us, some of whose stories are shared in this book.

Thanks to Jabulani Mhlanga for creating the web page, film clips and additional resources.

And thanks to our whole staff team, volunteers and prayer team at ROC.

Introduction

Earthly mountains speak of God's creative majesty. The very sight of them takes our breath away. You can scale a mountain, ski down a mountain. Or just scare yourself by thinking about such things! One thing's for certain – you couldn't contemplate moving a mountain. Even with a fleet of JCBs and a million men. And yet Jesus chose this tantalizing image to illustrate the truly unlimited potential available to those who follow him.

The toughest challenges we face in our lives, the biggest obstacles, the most seemingly insurmountable problems can be tackled, defeated and shifted by faith-fuelled prayer.

Relational struggles, financial strangleholds, emotional strife; whatever your mountain may be, through prayer, God's power can move it.

And not only at the personal level either – the huge challenges that cast their shadows across our communities can also be addressed through prayer. This book will inspire you with real-life examples and case studies.

> 'Truly I tell you, if you have faith as small as a mustard seed, you can say to this mountain, "Move from here to there," and it will move. Nothing will be impossible for you.' (Matthew 17.20)

Got anything in your life that seems impossible? A mountain in the way? Are you praying about it? Anything in your life right now you're concerned about that's really big? Like, mountain-sized big? You know, the type of thing that makes you step back, gasp a little, and just think to yourself, 'It can't be done'?

This book explores how prayer is able to move mountains in our lives. As we learn about prayer and experience answers to prayer, our faith grows – which leads to breakthrough times not only in our lives but in the places where we are called to serve.

1

Establishing your base camp

He replied, 'Truly I tell you, if you have faith as small as a mustard seed, you can say to this mountain, "Move from here to there," and it will move. Nothing will be impossible for you.' (Matthew 17.20)

Before we think about the mountain let's spend a little time reminding ourselves of the mover; who God is, what he's like and how he relates to us.

Our 'mountain' is a speck of cosmic dust to him. He can and will do whatever it takes to help us because of his love for us.

He tends his flock like a shepherd:
    he gathers the lambs in his arms
and carries them close to his heart;
    he gently leads those that have young.
Who has measured the waters in the hollow of his hand,
    or with the breadth of his hand marked off the heavens?
Who has held the dust of the earth in a basket,
    or weighed the mountains on the scales
    and the hills in a balance?

(Isaiah 40.11–12)

All we need is the tiniest amount of trust in him to spark our prayers.

On my desk right now is an actual mustard seed, a tiny thing. Its fragility serves to magnify the mightiness of God. My mustard seed is a permanent prompt that points me to the immeasurable power and love of Father God. It's a reminder that all I need to do is turn the mountain over to him and let him deal with it in his way. Sounds simple, doesn't it? That's because it is! We need to keep returning to the core of this truth, especially if we've been on a faith journey for many years. Mountain-moving prayer starts with childlike faith.

Simple faith

I became a Christian in 1980, just six months after getting married to Frank. I was looking for something to fill an empty void in my heart and my head which I had become aware of in my late teens. A few months later Frank also gave his life to Christ. We joined a small church with a strong emphasis on studying the Bible and we caught the bug. Thinking I should try and catch up with the rest of the congregation, who had mostly been brought up in the church, we both began to read ten chapters a day.

I especially loved reading the Gospels and I found the miracles of Jesus so compelling. In 1981 Frank and I went off for the weekend to Capernwray Bible College in Lancashire with two long-standing members of the church. We had a great faith-building weekend.

On the way home, late in the evening, just a few miles from the college and 100 miles from home, we had a punctured tyre in our old Renault 12. We did have a spare but it too was flat (long story – but basically this was our second puncture in 24 hours!). 'So what do you do at times like this?' we asked our more mature Christian friends in the back of the car. Eagerly I added, 'I believe we should pray and God will provide', such was my simple, childlike faith. They were less convinced but agreed to give it a go in the absence of other options, apart from hitch-hiking. 'Let's PUSH,' I said (Pray Until Something Happens). New Christians can occasionally be a bit overenthusiastic!

Anyway, we prayed. Frank then got out of the car. It was a deserted, dark road but after a few minutes headlights appeared in the distance.

The car slowed and then stopped. Then the miracle sequence began: the car that stopped was an old Renault 12. The driver was a kind and generous guy who offered to lend us his spare wheel and helped us deal with the pit stop in the pouring rain. But how would we get the wheel back to this angelic being? We were still two or three hours away from our home in Manchester. 'We'll find a way,' he said, and he wrote down his address. It was a mile or so from where we lived!

The funny side of this was how unsurprised we were and how

surprised our friends were. I look back now and chuckle. I can't say that prayer always works that way. But we were learning how to trust God and ask him to be in our everyday lives.

Early in our walk with Jesus, many find this simple faith fairly straightforward – we have the naive faith of children who trust their parents. Jesus' words about having the faith of a child in Matthew 18.3 are actually very challenging. A child had limited status in Israel. Children only had to pray once a day, whereas men were expected to pray three times. Jesus reframes faith using the example of the humble child. And that is not all. The relationship between us and God is also reframed in the Lord's Prayer. The use of the word Abba in the Our Father line uses a familiar family term for father, but not one that was often heard in worship and prayer. We are encouraged to trust.

But that simple faith has to contend with the realities of life. I can honestly say, as a Christian of 30-plus years, I've now got a lot more questions! When I share some of my vulnerabilities on the platform I have many conversations with people who are quietly going through hell on earth. We won't avoid those conversations in this book; we'll take hold of the realities of tough times and difficult circumstances in Chapter 4.

As we grow in the journey of faith we'll discover some key foundations for mountain-moving prayer. Often these principles only become apparent after a mountain has actually been moved and we find ourselves reflecting on how exactly God did it for us. These are valuable lessons that can help us develop a more confident approach to tackling obstacles. But remember to look for the evidence of that little seed of faith; you may not have been consciously exercising it at the time or, and this happens a lot, someone else in your circumstances may have been the faith agent when you were at your lowest point.

No easy answers

A few years ago I found myself in a spiritual void; I was in an emotional turmoil, caught between tears, anxiety and sorrow. Our 17-year-old son Josh had been arrested. He was alone in a cell. We couldn't see him yet. Your thoughts chase each other at a time like that. What would we say to him when we saw him? How would the situation resolve? How did this happen?

I was in a mess. Frank and I were preachers and church leaders. I had become known in the wider church community for my work with the Redeeming Our Communities movement (ROC). ROC works extensively with the police to reduce crime.

But Josh was becoming part of the problem. He had started to fall away from God when he was about 16. It was quite major. He was involved with a really bad crowd and with the antisocial behaviour that was part of their identity. As parents we were experiencing all the emotions you sometimes feel when you are parenting adolescents. It felt as if the devil was getting in our faces and taunting us.

It was no small thing. Josh was becoming very angry, had dropped out of college and was working at a call centre. He was out every night drinking and just seemed to be having a complete personality change.

It came to a head one day when the police came knocking at our door. Josh had been caught smashing up shops in the village where we live. His friends had run away but he was caught and arrested. He was taken several miles away to a police station and we could not see him for at least 48 hours.

I needed this mountain to move, but it took someone else to remind me of what I needed to do. I was really shaken, just wondering what on earth was going on. My daughter Sarah is a worship leader. She called round at the house and saw how upset I was. She reminded her mum of the priority of prayer and worship during times of trouble like this. At first I was a bit shocked about my own daughter reminding me about things I had taught her, in the way that our children can sometimes do!

The voice of God

She took hold of me and steered me into the front room and we began to worship and pray. Prayer and worship are tools of warfare, she said! We sang some songs in faith and called out to God. I got out my

4

prayer journals and reflected and prayed about the prophecies that we'd had for Josh when he was dedicated, as a child and growing up. I 'went into the enemy camp' as it were and claimed my son back as an act of faith. To be honest, I was still completely out of my depth but holding on to God.

On the Monday morning, Frank went to Josh's court hearing. Because it was a first offence he was given a conditional discharge but had to wear a tag for three months. He came home, and when he walked through the door I could see that he had changed. His whole demeanour was different. He fell to his knees in the hallway and said: 'I'm so sorry. Can you forgive me?'

I told him straight away: 'You're my son; I'm always going to forgive you, but what's happened to change you?' He explained that in the police cell he got on his knees and said to God: 'Please give me another chance. I'm going to serve you the rest of my life and I'm going to go and tell other young people all about you.'

He then told us he had one of those moments where the police cell felt flooded with the presence of God. And he thanked me for singing outside his cell. He heard my voice and another voice singing. I had to tell him that I wished I could have been there but hadn't known where he was and that we were not nearby singing. In fact we were five miles away. He was adamant that he had heard me and one other voice.

It suddenly occurred to me that what our heavenly Father had done was to communicate our worship and prayers to Josh so that he wasn't afraid, because he now knew his family were around him. He recognized our voices, but it was the voice of God he heard.

God had moved my mountain and would bring to pass all the promises that had surrounded Josh as he grew up.

Life wasn't all plain sailing after that, however. Quite soon afterwards, Josh lost his job because of the tag he had to wear. I eventually took him into work with me to help out, so that he was not lying in bed all day. At the time I had offices at The Message Trust, a charity in Manchester. One day Josh was helping out and he bumped into Tim Owen who ran a creative year-out performing arts course, Genetik Academy. Tim said to Josh, 'I just feel like I've got to offer you the opportunity to come on an internship with us on the course.'

It was already fully subscribed, but Tim urged him to come to an audition 30 minutes later so they could confirm he had the creative skills the course needed.

So he ran off quickly to learn a Lionel Richie song. He passed the audition and got offered the internship. Six months later, Andy Hawthorne, CEO of The Message, said to us, 'I think your son is an evangelist!' He set up a band called Twelve24, and ten years later they are travelling the world reaching thousands of young people. The band has recently been renamed Social Beingz.

God taught me so much through that experience about trusting him and about the power of prayer in times of trouble. Josh has given me permission to share his story, and it has given courage to other parents and grandparents. He now has a lovely Christian wife and three gorgeous children.

As many parents know, it feels terrifying when your children go away from the Lord. When I tell this story at conferences hundreds of people come forward to pray about their own situation. I tell them, 'You're not on your own in this, God is with you. You can't be with your kids twenty-four-seven, but God can.' I always felt that Josh was meant to be an evangelist even as a small child. We could see the plan God had for his life, but then he got hijacked for a period of time. This stressful and worrying experience taught me so much about prayer.

We all need our mountains to move – mountains in our families, in our self-esteem, at work, in our communities. Prayer can play the key role in all these settings, especially in helping people find their destiny.

Believing God desires good for us

Back to the Mover for another base-camp principle. There is a difference between agreeing with the notion that God is on our side and actually believing it in an attitude-shaping way. Mountain-moving prayer begins right here. God really does want the very best for us and is able to provide it – as long as we sow that little seed of faith into our prayers. Seeing is not believing. Seeing is seeing. Believing is demonstrating your dependence on God by your attitude and actions when you're standing at the foot of the mountain. Believing is seeing the mountain as an obstacle to the blessing that God desires for you.

> 'Which of you, if your son asks for bread, will give him a stone? Or if he asks for a fish, will give him a snake? If you, then, though you are evil, know how to give good gifts to your children, how much more will your Father in heaven give good gifts to those who ask him!'
>
> (Matthew 7.9–11)

These verses capture a persistent theme. In John 14.27, Jesus says, 'Peace I leave with you; my peace I give you.' His peace is more than a feeling – it's a comprehensive expression of his desire for us in every part of our being.

The original word translated as 'peace' is *shalom*. Like many Hebrew words, it has many shades of meaning. These include *peace, harmony, wholeness, completeness, prosperity, welfare* and *tranquillity*. This is the will of God that we seek to live out and embody.

It's a core thread in the gospel message. Jesus sends out the disciples with instructions to declare the peace of God for the houses they visit (Luke 10.5). Paul tells the Colossian disciples: 'Let the peace of Christ rule in your hearts, since as members of one body you were called to peace' (Colossians 3.15).

With God, it's grace first. He offers us his wholeness and calls us to abandon our rebellion and brokenness. Many of us carry around an image of God that involves him being slightly grumpy most of the time and really annoyed the rest. It is hard to pray to that version of God! So, as we come to pray, we stand on the rock of God's revealed character and make it our base camp: God wants to shine his face upon us (Numbers 6.25).

Abundant life

Now, while we're enjoying the implications of this truth, let's be careful not to miss something hugely important. Many Christians love to quote the declaration of Jesus recorded in John 10.10 where he compares his goals with those of the devil: 'The thief comes to steal and kill and destroy.' We don't need to look far for evidence of this in our world, even in the communities around us; but 'I have come that . . .'

Wait – let me ask you to say what you think the next single word is in this verse. Don't think for too long about it, just say out loud what pops into your head.

I wonder if you said 'you' – did you? Is that how you've internalized this promise: 'I have come that you may have life, and have it to the full'?

Well done if you said 'they', because that's correct. Of course God wants us to enjoy the abundance of life that Jesus brings, but it's not just for us. Jesus came to 'seek and save the lost'. To bring shalom to the victims of the thief. 'I have come that they may have life, and have it to the full.'

Here's an even bigger mountain we need to address – the social disintegration of community life in our civilized world. I'll say a lot more about this later in the book, but I wanted to point it out here because one of the base-camp elements is that prayer changes us. Don't be surprised if you begin to feel some of the pain in the heart of God for the conditions that others are living in. Don't be surprised if your personal mountains begin to diminish in comparison to those of others.

The late Jim Graham, Pastor of Goldhill Baptist Church in Buckinghamshire and internationally renowned Bible teacher, loved to challenge Christians with this: 'Prayer is not about us getting God on our side to solve our problems – it's more about God getting us on his side to serve his purposes in the world.' Yes, he will move our personal mountains but we mustn't stop there. His goal is to transform the lives of those around us as well – many of whom are as far away from living life to the full as it's possible to get.

His steadfast love, our persistent prayer

'His steadfast love endures forever' (Psalm 136.1, ESV). This refrain is repeated throughout Psalm 136 as the psalmist explores and recounts the history of God with the people of Israel, noting that his love and mercy endure for ever.

That history was not always easy or smooth but a belief in

the steadfast love of God sustained many through dark times. Preparation for being a people who will engage in mountain-moving prayer cannot ignore these hard times.

As I preach in towns and cities around the United Kingdom I hear many tragic stories about health problems and broken relationships. We can often empathize and recognize the anger or disbelief that can come upon us all in the hard-knock times of life. We recognize the internal conflict that caused a father to cry out to Jesus, 'I do believe; help me overcome my unbelief!' (Mark 9.24). He was not allowing his situation to snuff out his belief. We will often need to do the same.

We'll explore this a little more when we look at Matthew 7 in Chapter 3 and seek to understand how we can pray faithfully and yet avoid an unhealthy triumphalism. But for the moment we want simply to establish some core principles.

Our lives will usually be guided by some key values or intrinsic beliefs. When I got married I was very clear that it was for better or for worse. I feel the same about our relationship with God. I may waver due to hard circumstances but I always return to reliance on God.

Tests, trials and trust

The cast of characters we find in the Bible are not living perfect lives, free from friction. The story of Job is a catalogue of pain. The writer of Ecclesiastes would not last two minutes in some of our churches – with his cries of woe and his constant allusions to the meaninglessness of life.

The book of Psalms is often helpful to us in this respect however. The steadfast love of God calls forth persistent prayer in the midst of trial. There is human honesty, anger and despair in many of these passages as well as a constant returning to trust in God. Take, for example, Psalm 13:

> How long, Lord? Will you forget me for ever?
>   How long will you hide your face from me?
> How long must I wrestle with my thoughts
>   and day after day have sorrow in my heart?
> How long will my enemy triumph over me?

> Look on me and answer, LORD my God.
>> Give light to my eyes, or I will sleep in death,
> and my enemy will say, 'I have overcome him,'
>> and my foes will rejoice when I fall.
> But I trust in your unfailing love;
>> my heart rejoices in your salvation.
> I will sing the LORD's praise,
>> for he has been good to me.

The psalmist trusts, rejoices in the beauty of salvation and reminds himself of his history with God.

In Psalm 42 the writer addresses himself rather than God and says:

> As the deer pants for streams of water,
>> so my soul pants for you, my God.
> My soul thirsts for God, for the living God.
>> When can I go and meet with God?
> My tears have been my food
>> day and night,
> while people say to me all day long,
>> 'Where is your God?'
> These things I remember
>> as I pour out my soul:
> how I used to go to the house of God
>> under the protection of the Mighty One
> with shouts of joy and praise
>> among the festive throng.
> Why, my soul, are you downcast?
>> Why so disturbed within me?
> Put your hope in God,
>> for I will yet praise him,
>> my Saviour and my God.

In the time of trial the psalmist remembers the activity of God and the people of the community of God, and he hangs on to hope. Our understanding of prayer will be helped if we think of it as a diamond with many facets. A final facet that will help us establish a strong base camp relates to understanding what God is doing throughout his Church at this time.

God breathing out in multiple ways

As we establish our prayer base camp we should know that we're not alone and that God has set in place fresh insights into praying for our locality, our community and ourselves. God is breathing out his word, his wisdom for living and the enabling of the Holy Spirit for such a time as this. It feels as if there's a quickening of his people and a much greater awareness of prayer. We have more diverse ways of expressing that, and people are finding themselves at home with creative corporate prayer as well as seeking personal intimacy with God.

We're not abdicating the responsibility for prayer to the few fervent intercessors. We're finding new prayer practices embedded in the prayer and worship within our churches.

I reflect back on some words I wrote in 1994 in the early days of setting up a city-wide prayer movement in Manchester:

> In our dreams and visions we see crime rates dropping, violence decreasing, drug dealers disappearing, prostitution declining and apathy diminishing. We see businesses booming, housing improving, schools flourishing, and hope rising. We believe this will only come about as a result of God pouring out his Spirit upon a church united in determination to seek his face.
>
> (Green and Green, *City-Changing Prayer*)

Church leaders told us that an unprecedented expression of unity had been birthed across all the streams and denominations as a fruit of our gatherings. Out of this came new and effective missional projects – notably, Message 2000 and Festival Manchester – which drew thousands of young people to Manchester for a week of social action and evangelism, with huge evening celebrations in the city's major music arenas. Andy Hawthorne said that none of this could have been possible without the prayer movement.

There were several other tangible fruits of our commitment to prayer.

- Crime in Manchester was reduced in the years that followed. We started a strategic relationship with Greater Manchester Police, which still thrives today.

- The BBC moved their headquarters from London to Salford and the first Media City in Europe was birthed.
- Over 200 churches from different denominations and streams began to work together.
- New ministries were birthed, such as Eden (an organization committed to loving communities back to life), Barnabus (a ministry to the homeless), Mustard Tree, Boaz Trust (an asylum-seeker support), N-Gage (working with kids excluded from school).
- New prayer expressions started, such as Prayerstorm and, more recently, Greater Manchester Prayer (2018), which attracts over 1,000 people to its gatherings.
- Festival of Praise, a New Year inter-church city-wide night of worship, attracting 7,000-plus each year.

Alan Scott, a Vineyard pastor with roots in Coleraine, but now in the USA, tweeted this recently:

> It's time for signs that bring life to the City. Signs of business thriving, adoptions rising, schools flourishing, agencies partnering, disused churches reopening, crime diminishing, prodigals returning, paralysed walking and Kingdom breaking in.
>
> (@Alan_Scott)

We'll say more about praying outward-focused prayers to see our communities transformed in later chapters. For now, let's remind ourselves that our calling as Jesus followers is to seek not only the presence of God in our lives (and all the benefits that brings to us as individuals, families and churches) but also the power of his Spirit to be agents of that transformation as we advance his kingdom through our actions.

2

Muscle memory

We've established a base camp for our mountain-moving prayer. We've dealt with some of the fear we may have about climbing the peaks of prayer. Now we need to equip ourselves for the task. To help us establish mountain-moving patterns of prayer we should explore some key principles that will help us think clearly and become more effective in prayer.

I found myself wondering why Jesus chose to use the illustration of a mustard seed to teach about faith. If all he wanted to refer to was size, then why not a grain of sand or a speck of dust? I imagine the illustration was intended to point to the organic nature of the seed and its inherent capacity for growth. A seed appears to be of little value, small and apparently insignificant. It looks inert and lifeless. I don't think it's any coincidence that Jesus employed the same illustration in one of the parables of the kingdom in Matthew 13, where he spells out the meaning very clearly: the kingdom of God grows like a properly nurtured seed – in fact, it has the genetic programming to develop into the largest tree in a garden. Similarly, our faith has the latent potential to develop into fuel for mountain-moving prayer.

'You can say to this mountain, "Move from here to there," and it will move. Nothing will be impossible for you.'   (Matthew 17.20)

Stretching exercises

The incident that precedes this proclamation describes how Jesus' disciples had hit a ministry mountain they were unable to overcome – the boy severely troubled by an evil spirit. We're not told any details about their attempts to help the boy and his father but Jesus

13

was able to drive out the demon with just a word. And his explanation suggests that his disciples' prayers lacked faith. His words were not a rebuke but an encouragement. They needed to learn how to plant their faith seeds and nurture them. It's not something you can generate by effort or energy; the seed of faith must germinate in good soil and grow. The mountain-moving potential is already there, it just needs to develop and grow.

The same incident is related by Mark in chapter 9 of his Gospel and, according to some of the earliest manuscripts, Jesus included fasting alongside prayer as the key to developing strong faith. What's abundantly clear is that mountain-moving prayer doesn't just happen; it's not some kind of off-the-shelf accessory we can claim when we start to follow Jesus. It needs to grow through deliberate and conscious exercise and practice.

As we pray about the things that concern us we learn to exercise faith and stretch our faith muscles.

The UK Olympic team have done well in recent years partly because they are coached to move away from bad athletic habits and then retrained for the best sequence of actions for their sport. The body instinctively starts to remember, and new muscle memory is formed. Prayer works the same way. We can start to be a people of faith and prayer. Our new prayer habits can become second nature to us as our 'prayer memory' is strengthened. We're sometimes loath to pray mountain-moving prayers because deep down we think we're stretching our faith beyond what we believe might happen.

So . . . what sort of prayer should we be praying? Does prayer work? Why do we pray? What causes us to pray? What do we pray about?

Surprising statistics

What do people pray about?

I was surprised to learn, from a ComRes survey for Tearfund published in January 2018, that more than half of British people pray. Twenty per cent pray regularly, double the number who go to church. Over 50 per cent pray sometimes. Many have no conventional religious belief as we would understand it. For many non-believers, it is an instinctive response to a crisis: 'Please, God.' Just under half of those who pray said they believed God hears their prayers, which suggests that most feel their supplications are not answered. Four in ten go further, saying prayer changes the world; a similar number say it makes them feel better, which interests me greatly – I've always believed that prayer changes the person doing it much more than we realize. I wish there was more attention given to this by preachers and Bible teachers.

Family tops the list of subjects of prayers at 71 per cent, followed by thanking God (42 per cent), praying for healing (40 per cent) and for friends (40 per cent). Among the non-religious, personal crisis or tragedy is the most common reason for praying, with one in four saying they pray to gain comfort or feel less lonely.

How do church people pray? They often pray about immediate concerns. I am grateful to my own church, Ivy Church, who recently offered a sermon series on prayer. They surveyed their members about personal prayer and categorized the prayer themes into four main categories:

1 for my children to know and love Jesus;
2 breakthrough in my job/career;
3 release from anxiety, stress and fear;
4 financial security and freedom.

I think these are fairly typical. During the year at Ivy Church – 2018 was our year of prayer – we have seen some massive mountains move in people's lives! And prayer moves more than just our personal mountains. If we started to list wider prayer themes, they would no doubt include world poverty, war, famine, prayer for governments and civic leaders. We would want to pray for lost people whose eternal destiny hangs in the balance. Yes, we have our own mountains to shift, but we need to intercede on behalf of others as well.

There are four things that will help us understand how we can pray mountain-moving prayer for others and why we should.

1 Start with their need

Jesus and his disciples met people at their point of need. This was often expressed in a desire for healing prayer: blind Bartimaeus calls out to him; the woman with the issue of blood touches the hem of his garment; the centurion calls for him to bring healing for his servant Mary and Martha seek his healing touch for their beloved brother Lazarus. There are many more stories.

We too will meet many people who have not quite grasped the finer points of systematic theology yet, but they are desperate for a touch from the King. Their motives are highly personal but deeply understandable. Jesus recognizes this reality in his mission instructions to the disciples in Luke 10.7 where he instructs the disciples that, after they have served with, eaten with and entered into community with people, they are to pray for their sick. After all that, they are to declare that the kingdom of God has come near to them.

All around the UK Christian people are recognizing this in their street witness. Prayer stations, healing on the streets, houses of prayer, prayer walls, prayer and blessing chairs, prayer spaces in schools – all are ways in which we connect with people at their point of need and at a time when they are ready to exercise a desperate faith to see their own mountain move.

2 Pray your passions

A friend of mine was listening to the old Motown song 'What becomes of the brokenhearted?' and felt that God asked him the same question. So he started to read around the subject and quickly discovered a wealth of material in the Bible, contemporary science and health literature. He and his wife helped start a weekly meal, which attracts up to 40 non-churchgoers a week, and they continue to think about ways that the church can offer the hospitality of God in their community and start to rebuild the broken walls of people's lives.

People who come report fewer doctor visits, new hope for the future and a delight in the peaceful atmosphere of the weekly event. Some become curious about church, and salvations and baptisms have started to happen. The whole project is immersed in prayer. Faith and works meet around a table. Their team are praying their passion for the broken-hearted. They have gone where 'their best prayer takes them' in their neighbourhood.

This is important because we can dream big before we've dreamed small if we are not careful. We can try and move the mountain before we've trained and practised in the foothills. We can be crushed by the weight of our expectations and the demands these put on us and others. We can try to work out how we can change the nation before we have even done a pilot project.

One young person certainly discovered the power of starting small and then was blown away by the results. Marika Jones, a 16-year-old girl from Dawlish Christian Fellowship, had on her heart to do something for the homeless people in her town. She began to pray and very soon started to purchase backpacks that she filled with everything someone might need for a night on the streets – clothing, toiletries, food and even a thermos of hot chocolate. Each bag was tailored for a man or a woman. Then she took them on to the streets to hand them out, offering to pray with the recipients in Jesus' name. The fledgling project took off, so Marika prepared more and more backpacks, until she needed help funding the scheme. So she wrote to the local Co-op supermarket and told them what she was doing.

They were so impressed by her efforts that they offered to adopt her as their charity of the year. Marika had no charity number or bank account, so the money was diverted, with the consent of the Co-op, to the local Christian Outreach Charity UCADD (United Christian Action in Dawlish and District). In October 2017 we were invited to run one of our community engagement events, a ROC Conversation, in Dawlish, and Marika was one of those who told her story to the gathered people of goodwill (Christians, people of other faiths and none, council leaders, police officers, all kinds of people who share a common vision to bless their community).

After she had finished speaking, I was approached by a local teacher who was also at the event. He had been very moved by her story and asked if they could make it the school charity project for the next academic year. Her small mustard seed of faith had started to grow into a tree. She had dreamed small at first and now a harvest was being reaped around her town. As Marika's dad has always taught her, 'Things happen when you pray and do stuff!'

My own experience of starting small has included some dramatic moments when God seemed to challenge me about believing that mountains could move for his glory. Back in 2002, in the run-up to the Commonwealth Games in Manchester, our prayer movement (which, after nearly ten years of growth, now included Christians from just about every denomination and stream) began to pray specifically for a fairly safe list of things: good weather (well, maybe not safe in our city!), safety for athletes and visitors, and so on. We set a date for a city-wide prayer gathering and started to look for a venue. Suddenly, our mustard-seed faith germinated and decided it wanted to become a tree!

It seemed obvious to try and locate the prayer gathering in a sports venue, and as we prayed we felt a major faith boost: 'Let's hold it at the Velodrome', the UK's national cycling centre and home to British cycling since 1994. It has a capacity of 3,500 and is situated literally across the road from the newly constructed City of Manchester Stadium, the main venue for the Commonwealth Games.

I rang the General Manager, Jarl Walsh, and I said, 'I want to book your venue for Christians to pray for the success of the Games.' He wasn't fazed, and said, 'I can probably give you a room.' I explained that I wanted the whole place and I was expecting thousands to come. Silence at the other end of the line. Then he said, 'OK, this sounds important. You can have it.' I suddenly realized that I hadn't asked the critical question – how much would it cost? He replied, 'I'm not going to charge you the commercial rate; you can have the whole stadium for £400.' It was a pretty big miracle, even at that stage, when you consider that one of the large churches we were considering using wanted to charge me more than £400!

A few days before the event, Jarl rang me to say that the cyclists had to train right up to the start of our event and was that OK? I said it would be great if they were there as folks were gathering. So we had Olympic cyclists swishing around the track during our prayer meeting, and I even managed to persuade Jarl to come.

We had also invited the Chief Executive of the Games, Frances Done. It was our practice to invite civic leaders, and leaders in the city, to our prayer gatherings. We interviewed her about how we could pray. She seemed to appreciate our support very much.

Following that night, a few interesting things happened. The next day, when I went to pick up some of our things, I had a chat with Jarl. He had been reading a Bible that someone had left behind and he had some questions. He was also really impressed with the event;

he said everyone was friendly and thoughtful. They had left the place spotless. He said he would be happy to work with us again, and a few years later we used the Velodrome for an event with the evangelist J John.

A couple of weeks later, I took a call from Frances Done's office. Could I possibly recruit a 300-strong choir to sing at the opening ceremony of the Games with Russell Watson? I said yes. After the call I started to wonder how we could make it happen. It was before the days of social media. But we had a fantastic network of churches who were used to working together. So just a few emails and phone calls later we had 500 people wanting to audition.

And so, the first people to set foot in the new stadium, apart from those working on the project, were the 300 Christians who came to rehearse ahead of the opening ceremony. Claiming Joshua 1.3, 'I will give you every place where you set your foot', we prayer-walked throughout the whole stadium! A few years later it became the home of Manchester City Football Club, who have reaped the benefits ever since!

Obviously that last comment was very tongue-in-cheek (although ours is very much a Manchester City household) but, since we're talking about praying your passion, I do want to recognize that, for some people, football is a passion that has been an effective route for prayer. I have a friend who is involved in a great football-based ministry, though I know he sometimes worries that it is not a spiritual ministry. But the Bible doesn't recognize a sacred/secular divide; the earth is the Lord's and everything in it (Psalm 24.1). We use his good gifts for worship or for idolatry, and those are the criteria by which they are weighed.

If ROC had started in or around 1880 we would have been standing shoulder to shoulder with the churches and charities that were doing some or several of the following: feeding children, starting schools, creating further education for teenagers, running breakfast clubs, building social housing, creating parks, opening hospitals and starting cricket and football clubs. These last included Southampton, Everton, Fulham, Aston Villa, Tottenham Hotspur, Manchester City and Queens Park Rangers. The list would later include Leicester City, Charlton Athletic and others. Urban mission was about faith expressed in works. It was rooted in a passion for dignity, justice and the possibility of salvation for many. You can read more in the book *Thank God for Football* by Peter Lupson.

Sometimes we can mistake our passion for a diversion or a lesser calling and miss this great opportunity to pray for what God has put in front of us. Offer your passion to God. You may have a unique opportunity to be part of the presence of God, imitating Jesus and being empowered by the Holy Spirit, in a sphere of society that you have a passion about.

The prophet Nehemiah also prayed his passions:

> They said to me, 'Those who survived the exile and are back in the province are in great trouble and disgrace. The wall of Jerusalem is broken down, and its gates have been burned with fire.'
> When I heard these things, I sat down and wept. For some days I mourned and fasted and prayed before the God of heaven.
>
> (Nehemiah 1.3–4)

The prophet is weeping not merely for the broken walls and fire-damaged doors but for everything that these events say about the people of God and their enemies, and for the impact of these tragedies on the everyday lives of the people. The destruction is not new, but God raises up a prophet to address it.

The prophet Jeremiah also calls the people to pray about what God desired:

> Also, seek the peace and prosperity of the city to which I have carried you into exile. Pray to the Lord for it, because if it prospers, you too will prosper. (Jeremiah 29.7)

This would not have been an easy prayer to pray for a people who would not have felt kindly towards their abductors and who wanted to return to their homeland. We may also find that God releases a passion within us that we wished he could have given to someone else. We may not have the faith to see that mountain move. But as a wise person has said, 'Let God's wow be bigger than your how.'

After a while we may wonder why we resisted, as his heart is revealed, his purposes emerge and his enabling of us becomes clear.

I'm also aware that sometimes we need to join in with other

people's passions. We're encouraging people to participate in community prayer around special dates, anniversaries and events. It means more to the community when we're praying about something that means something to them. *Carry the burden, share the burden.*

God often raises up people who will enable others to pray about the big mountains. We can't all process all the information there is about problems in our communities or in the world. I have a friend who has a day job but also spends time seeking to understand the issues that lie behind human trafficking. They do the deep digging and give the rest of us information that can help us act and pray.

Being aware that we can't do everything, pray about everything and know everything will help keep us balanced, informed by people we trust and praying strategically. I believe that God has spoken to me about how communities can be redeemed. I focus on that and share what I discover. Maybe as you read you know there is a mountain that you can address in prayer, but can also help others understand.

3 Pray with a positive focus

One thing that saddens me greatly is the amount of negativity expressed in some Christian circles. Yes, there are many problems in our world, and many strange attitudes and opinions we're exposed to through the media and just our everyday lives. Some aspects of society do seem to be opposed to God's values and Christian ideals, but we need to be careful not to earn a reputation for being against things that we don't agree with. Why not focus on the positives and applaud things we see in society that are in line with our values? We always try to do this when we're praying for the city.

One example is how we pray for people in authority. MPs, city councillors, police chiefs, church leaders, business leaders – at our prayer gatherings we often invite high-ranking people to attend, and when we interview them we make a point of thanking them for their service. In many cases this has surprised them and often leads to a few tears. One strong example of positive prayer on a large scale was when we held a special evening of prayer for Greater Manchester Police. As always, the Chief Constable was being criticized in the media for some mistakes that had been made. We made no mention of this. Instead we prayed blessing on him, thanked him and all his officers for their sacrificial commitment to protect the population, and led the whole assembly in an extended time of raucous applause.

We then gave out hundreds of A3 posters and asked everyone to take them into their local police station to be posted on the canteen wall. Here's what the poster said:

We would like to say a big
THANK YOU

to all police officers and civilian employees
of Greater Manchester Police.
Thank you for serving our society with commitment,
diligence and integrity.
Thank you for affording protection to the vulnerable and
for your efforts to maintain law and order for the
benefit of all people in our region.

We are praying for you:

- That God would be with you in your work and in your leisure.
- That He would protect you and your families from evil.
- That you would know Christ's peace in your hearts and minds.

With love and appreciation on behalf of
the whole Christian Community of Greater Manchester.

4 Ask for redemptive revelation

Years ago we came across the principle of redemptive revelation and began to take this approach wherever possible. We'll say more later, but here is the core principle.

Where there is no vision [no redemptive revelation of God], the people perish; but he who keeps the law [of God, which includes that of man] blessed (happy, fortunate, and enviable) is he.

(Proverbs 29.18, AMPC)

When we began ROC we were speaking about redemptive revelation. We were believing that a change in our city was possible. We were looking on our city as a place that God wanted to bless, when it might have been tempting to look on it as lost and in need of judgement. We were praying for the wisdom of God to prevail there.

We started to see answers to prayer quite quickly. Our after-school ROC Café youth clubs were started in Manchester in 2008 because we had been praying about youth antisocial behaviour and youth crime. In the first year we saw youth crime drop on average by 40 per cent in areas where we had ROC Cafés. A couple of years ago the *Manchester Evening News* reported that antisocial behaviour had dropped by 90 per cent in Winton, Salford, around the area where we had a club. The photograph they printed in the paper showed Fr Ian Hall from St Mary's Church with some of the volunteers who were in their eighties! The project was a great example of partnership between the church, City West Housing and Greater Manchester Police. As more volunteers were needed, the youth worker from the nearby Lighthouse Church, Jesse Willis, came to the rescue with a bunch of willing helpers!

We record our regular ROC prayer meeting so that we capture what God might be saying and so that we can accurately reflect on that. For example, we were recently praying about finance, and phrases such as 'the bank of God' and 'the treasury of heaven' emerged as we prayed. In the weeks that followed, three large donations came from various sources, including one from a hedge-fund investor in the financial world!

There's a call to action that God gives when we pray. We're told to ask, seek and knock. So how does that work out in our everyday prayer lives?

3

Knock knock

———◦│◦———

> 'Ask and it will be given to you; seek and you will find; knock and the door will be opened to you. For everyone who asks receives; the one who seeks finds; and to the one who knocks, the door will be opened. Which of you, if your son asks for bread, will give him a stone? Or if he asks for a fish, will give him a snake? If you, then, though you are evil, know how to give good gifts to your children, how much more will your Father in heaven give good gifts to those who ask him! So in everything, do to others what you would have them do to you, for this sums up the Law and the Prophets.'   (Matthew 7.7–12)

As our muscle memory develops, the small steps of faith we take will soon grow into big persistent steps and strides of faith and prayer. And mountain-moving prayer will arise when faith for the seemingly impossible becomes part of the pattern of our thinking and the everyday patterns of our lives.

I want to focus on persistence in prayer in this chapter because mountain-moving prayer is often a long-term affair. One of the first sermons I heard as a young Christian was an exposition of this passage of Scripture and I can still remember the preacher explaining that the original grammatical construction was based on the present continuous tense. So 'ask' could be read as 'ask and keep on asking'; 'knock' as 'knock and keep on knocking'; 'seek' as 'seek and keep on seeking'.

When we understand this, it throws a different light on the whole practice of prayer. It's also fairly logical, isn't it? You keep knocking if you know there's someone home, especially if it's someone you love and urgently want to speak to. If you're looking for something you need and can't find it immediately you don't shrug your shoulders and forget about it, you keep on seeking.

The point is that God calls us to persistent prayer – may test our commitment, to see how important our relationship him really is, or to find out how much we want to see the moun move. Or maybe to allow us time to get our desires in line with his. Sometimes the door isn't answered quickly because we're asking for something that's not in line with his will and purpose. More later about these points. First, let's take a step back and remind ourselves again that our primary focus must be on the Mover rather than the mountain.

Ask

Here's the simple unvarnished truth: God wants to bless you! He's your heavenly Father and he desires to give good things to his children! Jesus tells us to ask and keep on asking. What you and I believe about who God is changes the way we pray. If we view him as a distant, slightly angry figure with a strong desire to reprimand us, then we will often pray tentatively and with a negative mindset because we're not praying in the light of his goodness, we're praying in the light of our worries, fears and unhealthy view of God.

We can become more confident in prayer as we start to believe we are praying in the right direction. Are we asking for things that reflect the character of God? His will is carried out in heaven, a place of bounty, beauty, creativity, goodness and celebration. Jesus tells us to pray that his will be done on earth too. Belief in the goodness of God will inform how we pray.

The stunning scope of his desire for all of us becomes focused on our individual lives when we consider Scriptures such as Psalm 139.13–18:

> For you created my inmost being;
>> you knit me together in my mother's womb.
> I praise you because I am fearfully and wonderfully made;
>> your works are wonderful,
>> I know that full well.
> My frame was not hidden from you
>> when I was made in the secret place,
>> when I was woven together in the depths of the earth.

Your eyes saw my unformed body;
> all the days ordained for me were written in your book
> before one of them came to be.
How precious to me are your thoughts, God!
> How vast is the sum of them!
Were I to count them,
> they would outnumber the grains of sand –
> when I awake, I am still with you.

How precious to me are your thoughts, God! Think along those lines. What are the thoughts of God? The Bible captures them for us but they can best populate our own imaginations when we meditate on the life and work of Jesus. And then we pray in the light of that.

Often we're praying about what God's intent is and what he would have us do:

> For we are God's handiwork, created in Christ Jesus to do good works, which God prepared in advance for us to do.   (Ephesians 2.10)

The reason that we can pray with confidence is found in what Jesus tells us about the Father in Matthew 7. If a pagan father knows how to care for his child, then how much more does God want to give good gifts to his children?

So from that place of confidence we become persistent askers, seekers and knockers. How else should we understand what Jesus meant by these words?

Ask, seek, knock: these three words imply distinct degrees of intensity. The New Living translation captures this well:

> 'Keep on asking, and you will receive what you ask for. Keep on seeking, and you will find. Keep on knocking, and the door will be opened to you. For everyone who asks, receives. Everyone who seeks, finds. And to everyone who knocks, the door will be opened.'
> (Matthew 7.7–8, NLT)

We can slip into praying to our Emergency God, but rarely speak to him outside those times of desperation. We wonder why we are not experiencing the lives we think we should have. If we're not careful we will neglect talking to the life-giver, but still expect to experience his favour.

> You lust and do not have. You murder and covet and cannot obtain.
> You fight and war. Yet you do not have because you do not ask.
>
> (James 4.2, NKJV)

Matthew 7 also calls us to be habitual prayer people. Jesus was speaking to a people who had a three-times-a-day tradition of prayer. At the Temple, prayer was undertaken 24 hours a day with the devout coming to Jerusalem twice a year, for a week, in addition to the big festivals, to be part of the every-minute-of-the-day praying. Jesus' call to keep on praying is echoed in Paul's call to the Corinthians to be filled with the Spirit (Ephesians 5.18). It was a calling to an old tradition of persistent prayer, invested with new meaning and focus.

Seek and find

What might we be seeking? Are we seeking God's will? Perhaps. Are we seeking his kingdom? Probably. But behind these two wonderful things will be our desire to seek his face.

> Look to the LORD and his strength;
> seek his face always.
>
> (1 Chronicles 16.11)

The Hebrew word for 'face' conveys a meaning to do with God's presence. We know that in the broadest sense his presence is everywhere. We're also aware that he has covenanted or promised to be with us. But we also know that his face becomes hidden to us by our own neglect, rebellion or indifference.

So the Scripture reminds us to seek his presence often. People today talk of being 'woke'. It's a concept arising from an African American expression, 'stay woke', which reflects the idea that people start to perceive the world in new ways as they grasp a key insight into social justice, politics or life. Are we 'woke' to the presence of God? Are we perceiving life through the lens of God expressed in Jesus and enabled in us by the Holy Spirit?

27

> If then you have been raised with Christ, seek the things that are
> above, where Christ is, seated at the right hand of God. Set your
> minds on things that are above, not on things that are on earth.
>
> (Colossians 3.1–2, ESV)

Seek the beauty of God, focus on that, stay woke to it so you can
minister to the brokenness on earth.

The presence of God becomes real to us in different ways but
it often has some common characteristics that will influence our
hearts and minds. God hears our prayers, but where prayer takes us
often changes us. We discover God in new ways quite often, as we
read the Scripture, pray personally and together, and as we hear the
word of God in prayer, testimony, teaching, preaching, singing and
conversation.

These activities are like theatres of the Holy Spirit where we
remind ourselves of truth, sing it, act it out and pray it as an expression of God at work in us. We hide the word of God within our hearts
through these things and it starts to remind us of his presence and
his desire to shine his face or presence upon us (Numbers 6.25).

When that happens, Numbers 6 tells us, grace and peace are released to us. And when they are released to us it brings the kingdom
of God near to people (Luke 10.9). God imparts his tender heart to
us when we meditate on him in this way.

Now, imagine what a tender-hearted generation could do. With
our hearts orientated towards God's intent and desire we then start
to knock on heaven's door, calling passionately for the release of
heaven on earth.

Knock

Jesus then said, 'Knock and the door will be opened to you' (Matthew
7.7). Here, the Lord uses a metaphor for prayer. If a person needs
something from someone behind a door, the most natural thing to
do is knock – and keep knocking until the door is opened and the
desire is met. In the same way, a believer should pray in faith for
God's provision and be persistent in prayer.

> Then Jesus told his disciples a parable to show them that they should
> always pray and not give up. He said: 'In a certain town there was a

28

judge who neither feared God nor cared what people thought. And there was a widow in that town who kept coming to him with the plea, "Grant me justice against my adversary."

'For some time he refused. But finally he said to himself, "Even though I don't fear God or care what people think, yet because this widow keeps bothering me, I will see that she gets justice, so that she won't eventually come and attack me!"'

And the Lord said, 'Listen to what the unjust judge says. And will not God bring about justice for his chosen ones, who cry out to him day and night? Will he keep putting them off? I tell you, he will see that they get justice, and quickly.'   (Luke 18.1–8)

Knocking denotes action. Faith that understands the character of God will overflow into action. When we are immersed in the story of who God is it shapes how we think about everything in our lives. We start to become imitators of God and feel compelled to do beautiful things in his name. Faith without works is dead (James 2.20). Faith with works is life-giving.

Asking, seeking, knocking prayer can become a habit of mind and heart, not just an activity for Sunday. Here's how the prolific Bible commentator Lawrence O. Richards explains it:

> Jesus describes prayer as asking, seeking, and knocking. 'Ask' is the act of prayer in its simplest form. 'Seek' conveys intensity, and 'earnest sincerity'. And 'knock' pictures persistence. We knock on the door of heaven and keep on knocking!
>
> It is important not to mistake what Jesus is saying as laying down conditions which, if met, will move God to respond to us. Jesus is not saying if you ask ardently enough, then God will answer your prayer. He is simply saying that when we feel a need so intensely that it drives us to the Lord again and again, we need not be discouraged even if the answer is delayed. God really does care about those things that matter to His children. And God responds to our requests by giving us good gifts.
>
> (Quoted in Nappa, 'Matthew 7:7–12; Ask, Seek, Knock')

Alongside the call to persistence we have just noted, we discover that prayer and faith bear fruit when they are rooted in assurance and submission.

Where prayer and faith meet

I want to show you from the Bible that faith prays in two ways: faith prays with assurance, and faith prays with submission. These two kinds of prayer are given to us for different situations. It is important that we know how to use them and that we learn to distinguish between them. The book of James tells us:

> Is anyone among you in trouble? Let them pray. Is anyone happy? Let them sing songs of praise. Is anyone among you ill? Let them call the elders of the church to pray over them and anoint them with oil in the name of the Lord. And the prayer offered in faith will make the sick person well; the Lord will raise them up. If they have sinned, they will be forgiven. Therefore confess your sins to each other and pray for each other so that you may be healed. The prayer of a righteous person is powerful and effective. (James 5.13–16)

Elijah was a man just like us. But he also had a kind of Godly audacity. James highlights him as one who prays bold prayers: 'He prayed earnestly that it would not rain, and it did not rain on the land for three and a half years' (James 5.17). Elijah must have been sure that what he prayed would happen because 1 Kings tells us Elijah went into the court of the tyrant, King Ahab, and said, 'As the LORD, the God of Israel, lives, whom I serve, there will be neither dew nor rain in the next few years except at my word' (1 Kings 17.1).

You have to be pretty sure of the answer to your prayer to speak like that to the King. I love this passage so much! There had been more than three years of drought. Elijah speaks prophetically that the rain is on its way. But then he goes up the mountain to pray. Although he knows rain will come, he still goes to pray. We can learn a lot from that.

Persistent prayer is also illustrated here. The servant is instructed to go to look for rain seven times. This is over a period of time. Elijah is still seeking God's face. When the answer eventually comes it's only a very small sign – a cloud the size of a man's fist. They are still waiting for the rain to come, but faith sees the sign however small. Do we dismiss the small signs God is sending our way?

And Elijah said to Ahab, 'Go, eat and drink, for there is the sound of a heavy rain.' So Ahab went off to eat and drink, but Elijah climbed to the top of Carmel, bent down to the ground and put his face between his knees.

'Go and look toward the sea,' he told his servant. And he went up and looked. 'There is nothing there,' he said.

Seven times Elijah said, 'Go back.'

The seventh time the servant reported, 'A cloud as small as a man's hand is rising from the sea.'

So Elijah said, 'Go and tell Ahab, "Hitch up your chariot and go down before the rain stops you."'

Meanwhile, the sky grew black with clouds, the wind rose, a heavy rainstorm came on and Ahab rode off to Jezreel. The power of the LORD came on Elijah and, tucking his cloak into his belt, he ran ahead of Ahab all the way to Jezreel.   (1 Kings 18.41–46)

How remarkable is the last verse? Ahab rode to Jezreel. Elijah runs ahead of Ahab's chariot! What's the difference? The power of the Lord comes upon him. When that happens he is able to run faster than the chariot. The distance between Mount Carmel and Jezreel is said to be around 30 miles!

Elijah knew that what he prayed would happen. That's how it happened when the rains returned, and I think it is reasonable to assume that it happened the same way three years earlier when the rains stopped. God told Elijah what would happen, and so Elijah prayed with great assurance (1 Kings 18.42).

In the great scheme of things it would not have been easy for Elijah to be so assured. But his assurance is rooted in his submission to God. He trusted the God who had helped in his journey of faith up to this time. He submitted any rational doubt to his belief in the supernatural power of God and the relationship he already had with him.

Prayer has the ability to usher in the power of the Lord when we do his exploits. You can find yourself receiving supernatural ability or strength to do kingdom exploits. As the prophet Isaiah says:

> Those who hope in the LORD
> will renew their strength.
> They will soar on wings like eagles;

Knock knock

> they will run and not grow weary,
> they will walk and not be faint.
> (Isaiah 40.31)

I'm reminded of the importance of committing everything to the Lord in prayer, especially when that thing seems difficult and I can't see a way forward. On many occasions it feels as though a heaviness is lifted and I experience the power of the Lord to enable me in a way I can't fully explain.

Persistent prayer people

One of the keys is simply believing that God is willing to help us with our kingdom activities. Here are what two saints from our praying past have said.

> Perseverance in prayer is not overcoming God's reluctance but rather laying hold of God's willingness. Our sovereign God has purposed to sometimes require persevering prayer as the means to accomplish His will. (Warren Weirsbe, quoted in Thrasher, *A Journey to Victorious Praying*)

> Some people think God does not like to be troubled with our constant coming and asking. The way to trouble God is not to come at all.
> I live in the spirit of prayer. I pray as I walk about, when I lie down and when I rise up. And the answers are always coming. Thousands and tens of thousands of times have my prayers been answered. When once I am persuaded that a thing is right and for the glory of God, I go on praying for it until the answer comes. George Müller never gives up! (George Müller, quoted in Parsons, *An Hour with George Müller*)

Persistent prayer is a habit we need to adopt. I like what Mark Batterson says when he reminds us to stop praying ASAP (as soon as possible) prayers, and instead start praying ALAIT (as long as it takes) prayers. This is biblical.

'AS LONG AS IT TAKES' PRAYERS
There's nothing wrong with asking God to move quickly (David prayed this all the time in the Psalms), there is a clear precedent

32

from Scripture that God not only works through our prayers, but He also works on us as we pray – and this often means it takes time, patience and persistence to see the answer come through.

The book of Daniel contains a powerful illustration of Daniel praying and fasting for three weeks, until an answer is given. The angel of the Lord tells him that as soon as Daniel started to pray, the answer had been given from heaven, but there was a war in the heavenlies that caused it to take longer to arrive. We often have no clue how much God is at work through our prayers!

Jesus actually taught us to pray like this. In Luke 18, Jesus tells his disciples a story 'To show them that they should always pray and not give up.' He goes on to explain the power of persistent prayer. God wants us to always pray, and not give up! Is there a prayer you've been praying, that you've recently given up hope on? Keep on praying! Jesus wants you to. He wouldn't have given us this story if he didn't.

We often want instant results from God, but God wants patience and endurance from us. It is difficult to overestimate the biblical importance of patience and endurance in maturing our faith. The Bible has a lot to say about this (see 2 Peter 1.4–8; Romans 5.3–5; James 1.2–4).   (Batterson, *Draw the Circle*)

Dave, who is helping me write this book, shared with me about his brother-in-law, David. He had turned his back on church in his teens. For more than 40 years people prayed for him but none as persistently as his parents, his sister and his business friend Frank. Frank prayed for him for 20 years. You have to think that many of us might have given up, but not Frank. One day several years ago Frank took David to church and God spoke through the children's talk. Later that day Frank had the incredible joy of leading his friend to Christ.

That persistent prayer bore fruit in more than one moment of conversion. David has helped establish the local Winter Night Shelter, a rehab house called 'The Bridge', a local branch of the national homeless project, Hope into Action, and a workplace skills project called Hope Woodwork. The fervent prayer of one man has been part of what God did to influence hundreds of lives.

How to pray persistently

1 Just do it

We are a diverse people. Many can carry information in their head, pray spontaneous prayers and pray up a storm. If that's you – just do it. And keep on doing it – that's persistence, right there!

2 Make a list

I keep a written record of the prayers that I'm praying in a journal and then reflect back on that journal. I can see a pattern of persistence in prayer, a pattern of change and a pattern of answers to prayer. The first step is giving yourself permission to pray the same prayer more than once. Keep calling on the name of the Lord and believing in the promise of his character that we find in those beautiful names – Prince of Peace, Wonderful Counsellor, Mighty God, and many more.

Some people make lists and put a small tick against each request as they return to it later.

3 Have a structured focus

Persistent prayer can often be facilitated by a structured focus. It can help us see the breadth of what God desires to bless and restore. The Ffald y Brenin retreat in Pembrokeshire has helped many see the creative possibilities of steady rhythms of prayer. Their seven days of prayer for your locality is helpful. Here is a version of it:

Here are seven simple prayer ideas that you could use this week. When praying you might like to use the following form of words:

I bless (that day's subject) in the name of Jesus and for his Glory. Bless them with peace, health and a revelation of God through Jesus. (You can expand on this – but it's a place to start.)

Take time to bless the friendships and activities of the place or person that you are blessing – asking God to bring his kingdom values to the awareness of those there. Sometimes it will

34

be appropriate to pray out loud, other times it will just be you and God talking to each other.

Monday
Bless your family members – both near and far.

Tuesday
Bless your workplace or the schools that your children might attend.

Wednesday
Bless the streets around where you live – if you can, walk around and quietly pray. Bless them with peace.

Thursday
Bless and pray for someone in your neighbourhood, whom you may see regularly and perhaps even exchange greetings with. Ask God for openings to talk further and pray for them personally.

Friday
Bless your enemies. Not easy – but biblical. Jesus reminded us to 'love your enemies, bless those that curse you, do good to those that hate you, and pray for those who spitefully use you, and persecute you' (Matthew 5.44, NKJV).

Saturday
Bless a Christian friend. Ask God to reveal his goodness to your friend in a fresh and new way.

Sunday
Bless the church. As you think about gathering with them today, ask God to bless his people and increase their witness to his love and grace.

The possibilities are endless with this approach. You could pray for the workplaces, courts of justice, schools, doctors' surgeries or hospitals, town hall, marketplaces and sports/parks spaces of your locality. Take one per day. See if these things can be found on a route you often use. Follow the basic pattern of prayer above.

What about schools – teachers, children, parents at the gate, governors, teachers' assistants, catering staff, caretakers, the headteacher?

Create a small A4 folded to A5 leaflet around these themes and give them to the relevant people in your church. Release persistent prayer through easy-to-use, focused prayer guides.

4 Use liturgy

Some of us shy away from liturgy. But we can miss the voice of God when we do this. We can also miss out on life-giving insights and the power of regularly reminding ourselves of truth. I find outward-facing liturgy helpful, such as that created by Shane Claiborne and his friends. Like me, Shane has a passion for cities, Jesus and prayer. His book *Common Prayer* could help you establish a pattern of persistent prayer. Sometimes the words crafted by others can help us as we seek to pray for diverse and different situations.

Here is a workplace prayer from *Common Prayer*:

> May God give his blessing on this place.
> God bless it from roof to floor,
> From wall to wall, from end to end,
> From its foundation and in its covering.
> In the strong name of the Triune God:
> All evil be banished,
> All disturbance cease,
> Captive spirits freed.
> God's Spirit alone
> Dwell within these walls.
> We call upon the Sacred Three
> To save, shield and surround
> This place, this day, and every day.

Amen and amen to all the above.

4

Quietly confident

———◆———

'In repentance and rest is your salvation,
in quietness and trust is your strength.'
(Isaiah 30.15)

One of the toughest challenges facing those who believe in the power of prayer has always been to explain why some mountains are moved quickly while others appear to stay right where they are. Theologians, scholars, pastors and evangelists throughout the ages have made contributions ranging from triumphalistic reduction-ism at one end of the scale to academic dismissiveness at the other, squeezing into short slogans the complex relationship between God's love, power and will and humankind's fallenness – or simply reject-ing completely any concept of divine intervention.

I'm not going to pretend to have 'the answer' but I do want to try to understand what is going on when God appears to withhold the response we're asking for. We went some way to appreciating this in the last chapter when considering the need to be persistent in our prayers, but there is still more to say.

Unshakeable truth

A number of truths need to be held in equal tension in order to maintain a biblically balanced position. We keep returning to the core of our faith, God's love for us, which means he always wants what's best for us. And we must add to this his unlimited power over everything, including evil in all its forms, which means he always has the ability to change anything that obstructs his will for our lives. Into the mix we need to sow that little organic seed of faith that needs to germinate and develop. And it's this last element that helps us to listen and learn from God during times of silence. We need to allow the opportunity for our faith to grow beneath the ground, quietly and invisibly, in the soil of our personal circumstances, watered by the Holy Spirit, developing the fruit that will colour our character and bear witness to the world.

Frank was talking to an elderly member of our church who told him that she was enduring some really tough circumstances; her husband had passed away a few months before and she had recently had some difficult health issues that had kept her housebound and lonely. He asked her how he should pray for her, and she replied, 'I want to make sure I learn whatever it is the Lord is teaching me through all of this.'

Sometimes we'll hear God say 'No' when we bring a specific request to him. Other times it might be 'Wait'. The important thing is not to allow our earthly view of what we're going through to modify our understanding of God. He does love us and he does want the best for us. He is able to do all things. But his ways are not our ways, and we need to trust him and discern what else we should be giving attention to. He hasn't left us; he's walking with us through the valley. The mountain we're looking at is sometimes the wrong one.

Wendy

I was on holiday with my family when I received the call. My friend and prayer partner of over 25 years was in hospital. The family had been gathered. A few weeks earlier she'd been with me on a trip to Belfast and I'd started to suspect something was wrong. She'd been getting headaches and wasn't eating much. She was initially diagnosed with a brain tumour but more tests would reveal that she actually had two tumours. Things weren't looking good and I desperately wanted to get back from holiday to see her. I went straight to the hospital, as soon as we got home. Imagine my surprise when I saw her sitting up in bed with a big smile on her face. The doctor came in and started to explain to her, the family and me that there was going to be surgery followed by treatment. While the doctor was talking, Wendy was quite distracted and seemed amused! After a lot of explanation the doctor left the room. I asked her, 'Did you understand what the doctor said?' and she responded, 'Well, it must be fine because no one cried!' Looking back, I feel that she was somehow lifted above the earthly situation into God's immediate presence. You often hear that people who are facing these kinds of huge mountains of pain and uncertainty say that they feel a strong sense of God being with them and a sense of the peace that passes all understanding.

She went through surgery, chemotherapy and stem cell replacement therapy over a period of about nine months. The treatment was gruelling. She lost her hair and nails and had no energy, but there was nearly always a smile on her face. She constantly shared her faith in Jesus with other patients and hospital staff. Her irrepressible personality remained unaffected in spite of the prolonged pain and discomfort she experienced – including a spell of solitary confinement that lasted four weeks (a major struggle for such an extrovert whose energy comes from human interaction).

Then, on 16 March 2018, she rang me to say the cancer had gone into remission. We have a big school bell in our ROC office which we always ring when we hear of answers to prayer and good news. The bell was ringing loud and clear that day.

Almost one year after the diagnosis, Wendy was back on the road with us when we went to run the ROC Conversation in Tavistock. On the way, we had a photo taken of Wendy and me next to the Tavistock road sign. This sign of God's grace sparked a huge number of good wishes via social media. Hundreds of people had been praying for her and were delighted to see her back in action. It had been a long nine months with a great ending. But it reminds us that we can't talk about mountain-moving faith without stepping aside to ask and answer the questions that flood our minds when it seems as if heaven is silent and suffering is prolonged.

A verse of Scripture I received when my mum was dying of cancer comes to mind 'Thou wilt keep him (her) in perfect peace whose mind is stayed on thee: because he (she) trusteth in thee' (Isaiah 26.3, KJV). Interestingly, I received this word of encouragement when reading in the King James Version, which I don't usually read, but my mum always did. God wanted to confirm very clearly to me that the word was for her. She was kept in his peace, quietly confident until she went to be with him on 13 December 2008.

There are three insights that may help us.

1 Do we want God or the stuff?

Pete Greig, a key figure in the 24/7 prayer movement that has touched over 90 nations so far, knows this only too well. Early in the development of their innovative prayer rooms his wife Sammi was found to have a brain tumour. As they walked through this dark valley he slowly pieced together a booklet that would later become a book: *God on Mute: Engaging the Silence of Unanswered Prayer*. He reminds us:

> God's great aim has always been, and will forever be, relationship with us. Sometimes, He may deprive us of some*thing* in order to draw us to Some*one*. And when we reciprocate – when we decide that we want Him more than we want His stuff – the most amazing thing happens. We are rewired and our requests are either altered as we grow to know and to prefer what He wants for us, or they are simply answered because, in seeking first the kingdom of God, 'all these things' are given to us as well (Matt. 6:33).
>
> (Greig, *God on Mute*)

The ancient story of Shadrach, Meshach and Abednego speaks to the type of commitment to God, for himself alone, that Pete mentions above. Daniel's three young friends are resolute:

> 'King Nebuchadnezzar, we do not need to defend ourselves before you in this matter. If we are thrown into the blazing furnace, the God we serve is able to deliver us from it, and he will deliver us from Your Majesty's hand. But even if he does not, we want you to know, Your Majesty, that we will not serve your gods or worship the image of gold you have set up.' (Daniel 3.16–18)

This principle can super-charge your prayer life! I know my God is able to do the impossible, but even if he doesn't, I will serve him and follow him only! This kind of praying offers supreme submission, faith and honour to God.

Dave's friend Jon prayed in this way as he dealt with a life-threatening sickness in his twenties – 'Either way I win.' He was praying for God to heal him, but he knew that eventually he would be fully restored and given a glorified body in heaven. All of us who trust in Christ can say as we pray, 'Either way I win.'

2 Lean on God's wisdom

I love this insight, again from *God on Mute*, from an unknown soldier about the nature of prayer and our interaction with God:

> I asked for strength that I might achieve;
> He made me weak that I might obey.
> I asked for health that I might do greater things;
> I was given grace that I might do better things.
> I asked for riches that I might be happy;
> I was given poverty that I might be wise.
> I asked for power that I might have the praise of men;
> I was given weakness that I might feel the need of God.
> I asked for all things that I might enjoy life;
> I was given life that I might enjoy all things.
> I received nothing that I asked for, all that I hoped for.
> My prayer was answered, I was most blessed.
>
> (Quoted in Greig, *God on Mute*)

It's not always easy to have the humility of this man who learned so much as he examined what he was praying for and why. But he reminds us that there will be times when we are too close to the issue to step back and see the deeper wisdom God may have for us.

It's also hard, with this in mind, to watch people wrestling with family illness, work issues or personal health challenges and not to try and shield them from it all: to urge them to have a simple and uncomplicated faith.

Frank and I wrestled with this over our son Josh, during that time I wrote about in the opening chapter; he was going around with an unhelpful group of friends and making poor decisions. Should we let him make his own mistakes and learn, eventually arriving at a grown-up, personally 'owned' faith? It's a good principle, but it's hard to implement because our instinct is to protect.

Sometimes growing in maturity and faith presents us with a dilemma. We have to work hard to understand and interpret Bible truths and think carefully about how to apply them. Often we may want to protect young Christians from things we think it will be hard for them at that point in their journey to bear. They may struggle if God says 'No' or 'Wait'.

Sometimes it takes time.

3 Wait patiently

There's a song we sometimes sing that explores what is happening as we wait upon the Lord. It encourages us to take courage and stay steadfast. They are not mere words artfully woven into a song, but express something of the heart cry of the psalmist:

> I waited patiently for the Lord;
> he turned to me and heard my cry.
> He lifted me out of the slimy pit,
> out of the mud and mire;
> he set my feet on a rock
> and gave me a firm place to stand.
> (Psalm 40.1–2)

Out of the mud and the mire. Some translations talk about the 'miry clay'. A little research suggests that what we call quicksand may also be in view in this passage. There's a profound discipleship prayer and faith-journey insight here.

If you consult a how-to guide on getting out of thick, wet clay or quicksand you're told not to thrash around, to take rests and be aware that 'slowly but surely' is the best method when making your way to the edge and getting back on firm land.

As we face challenging circumstances in our lives it can be tempting to think that our answers will be instant and our restoration will be quick. The image of someone being slowly but gently lifted up so that they can find a firm place to stand will, however, echo the experiences that many of us have had. It's not easy to have the patience and endurance we need, but these two character traits are the fruit of the Spirit captured by the words 'longsuffering' or 'forbearance' in Galatians 5.22–23. We're not alone as these situations unfold and we can ask for the Holy Spirit's enabling.

This is where we see a quiet confidence unfolding. Sometimes when we experience trials we can feel and know that God has found us and knows our need, but the rescue takes time. We just have to be patient and calm.

I love these verses from James:

> Consider it pure joy, my brothers and sisters, whenever you face trials of many kinds, because you know that the testing of your faith produces perseverance. Let perseverance finish its work so that you may be mature and complete, not lacking anything. (James 1.2–4)

The Greek word for 'many kinds' literally means 'multi-coloured'; the same word is used in 1 Peter 4.10 to describe God's grace; so, for every particular trial we experience there is a specific 'colour' of grace to match it.

Jesus never seems to have run anywhere. His slow but steady walking, and his willingness to give grace and healing along the way to others, must have been frustrating for the centurion awaiting the healing of his servant, or for Mary and Martha as they saw their brother Lazarus die while they awaited Jesus. But their answer was coming and they could, and we can, be confident in the wisdom and power we find in Jesus and his embodiment of the heart of God.

As I write this, it's just a few weeks since a group of 12 young Thai boys and their football coach were pronounced missing, feared dead, following a massive rainstorm that flooded an underground cave network they'd been exploring as part of an end-of-season trip. The world held its collective breath for days while search and rescue divers risked their own lives to try and find them. Suddenly, the news broke: the boys had been found alive but trapped in a snaking system of caverns and crevices, which posed a range of problems for rescuers; a precarious situation deep in the bowels of the earth. Wonderful news, we all thought. Soon they would be reunited with their families and all would be well. Expert divers, including a doctor, were able to take food and other supplies to the boys who were frail and weak after nine days spent in darkness and with very little food. While they gradually built up their strength, rescue plans were discussed. The route they took to enter the caves had been treacherous even before the heavy rain; some of the narrowest tunnels through which they wriggled were now filled with water. Even the experienced

43

divers had to take many hours to negotiate a way through – one died when his air supply failed.

It took another week before it was possible to bring them back through the flooded caves. The battle to preserve the little air they had in their subterranean sanctuary was a constant one, with water finding its way into the caves as quickly as it was pumped out. The final four boys emerged to jubilant celebrations after 18 days underground.

I can see many parallels when it comes to the situations we find ourselves in. Struggling with ill health, addictions, oppression, feeling trapped and unable to see any way out, may leave us feeling hopeless and lost. Will we be rescued? How long will it take? Will it be complicated? God, in his wisdom, knows how to rescue us at times like this, but it's not always quick and straightforward. We have to learn to trust his judgement.

> My trust is in you, O LORD;
> you are my God.
> (Psalm 31.14, GNB)

This is quiet confidence. There's a big difference between this and being triumphalistic.

There are those who will claim that we need to have an unwavering faith and only speak positively about our future outcomes. This is not a quiet confidence that allows for our human frailty – it's an unreal attempt to manufacture a positive mental attitude, a type of superstition that can leave us confused and disappointed. Why didn't God answer? Did we have enough faith? Did we pray enough? Is there sin in my life preventing God from acting for me? Did we pray the right prayers?

The biblical character who can help us find wisdom and quiet confidence is Job. He often dialogues with God. Writer Bob Hostetler offers a framework that can help us understand how the prayers of Job can help us today. Here are five key points based on his insights.

1 Be transparent. Job had an honest dialogue with God. He spoke about his pain and anguish, asking God for relief from his terrors and complaining loudly. 'I will give free rein to my complaint and speak out in the bitterness of my soul' (Job 10.1). 'Stop frightening me with your terrors' (Job 13.21). 'Surely, God, you have worn me out' (Job 16.7).

C. S. Lewis reminds us that, we too must learn to 'lay before Him what is in us, not what ought to be in us' (*Letters to Malcolm*).

2 Ask God to speak. Who is doing all the talking when we pray? Maybe God has correction, guidance or affirmation for us. Job asked God to speak, praying things such as: 'Tell me what charges you have against me' (Job 10.2); 'Show me my offence' (Job 13.23).

So pray like Job. Ask God to speak to you.

3 Keep asking. Job is not a short book. But part of the beauty of the story and the poetry is Job's persistence. He grows desperate (and angrier), but he never gives up. As we've seen, Jesus also urges us towards persistence in prayer: keep on asking, and you will receive what you ask for (Matthew 7.7). So pray like Job. Keep asking.

4 Accept correction. When God finally does speak, Job says, 'I put my hand over my mouth. I spoke once, but I have no answer – twice, but I will say no more' (Job 40.4–5). Job wanted God to answer him, but when he finally does, God says, 'I will question you, and you shall answer me' (Job 40.7).

That's not easy to hear, but Job, to his credit, bowed low and accepted God's correction. And so should we.

5 Keep waiting. In the midst of his heart-breaking trial, Job's wife encouraged him to 'curse God and die!' (Job 2.9). But he persisted, as we discover in the 40 chapters that follow. He waited and he endured. And eventually, the Bible says, 'The LORD blessed the latter part of Job's life more than the former part' (Job 42.12).

So pray like Job. But wait, too. Remember that God's time

zone is different from yours. He may not show up according to your schedule, because sometimes the waiting is as much a part of his plan for you as the destination.

It's very rare for anyone to go through all the suffering Job experienced. In fact some Bible commentaries suggest that he experienced the fullest possible range of suffering known to humanity. We can only perhaps relate to some of what he went through but it certainly serves to teach us about trusting God.

We're staying with this theme of persistence, waiting and quiet confidence because it feels real and true both to the biblical accounts and to our own experience.

Paul speaks of

> great endurance; in troubles, hardships and distresses; in beatings, imprisonments and riots; in hard work, sleepless nights and hunger; in purity, understanding, patience and kindness; in the Holy Spirit and in sincere love; in truthful speech and in the power of God; with weapons of righteousness in the right hand and in the left; through glory and dishonour, bad report and good report; genuine, yet regarded as impostors; known, yet regarded as unknown; dying, and yet we live on; beaten, and yet not killed; sorrowful, yet always rejoicing; poor, yet making many rich; having nothing, and yet possessing everything. (2 Corinthians 6.4–10)

God doesn't absolve us from the hard times we encounter in a fallen world. But he walks with us through the dark valleys:

> Even though I walk
> through the darkest valley,
> I will fear no evil,
> for you are with me;
> your rod and your staff,
> they comfort me.
> (Psalm 23.4)

This Davidic psalm is part of a trilogy. Psalm 22 is called a messianic psalm as it speaks of the suffering of Jesus and his death. In Psalm 23 Jesus is the good shepherd, and in Psalm 24 he is the King of glory. Psalm 23 refers to the present and Psalm 24 to the future.

That's the order in which God ministers to us. Jesus died first so that we would have a saviour to redeem us. We discover him as the good shepherd as he ministers to us in our time of need. One day we will reign with him in glory.

The rod and staff are used by a shepherd in tending the sheep. The shepherd's staff is a long slender stick with a crook on the end. When tired, a shepherd leans on the staff. He will use it to return a lamb to its mother. Sheep see the shepherd use the rod and staff to protect, guide, lead and to get them out of trouble and away from dangerous paths.

The prophet Isaiah also speaks of the promise of God that he will be with us in our hour of need: 'When you pass through the waters, I will be with you' (Isaiah 43.2).

We take the long view when faced with suffering. Paul told the Philippians about 'being confident of this, that he who began a good work in you will carry it on to completion until the day of Christ Jesus' (Philippians 1.6).

These hard times are when we often feel the least like praying. In those moments, the enemy wants to disempower us and tell us we are defeated. We may be ministering to people but still struggling in our marriages, in our families, or facing brokenness in our health. Our trust is in him not in our own abilities, energy or skills. Our faith is growing and even our most feeble prayers will see the mountain move.

Justin Welby, the Archbishop of Canterbury, told a BBC reporter that he has struggled at times with what he calls 'the black dog' – a phrase Winston Churchill used to describe episodes of depression. In 1983, the Welbys lost a 7-month-old baby, Johanna, in a car crash. Twelve months later, another of his children was critically ill. It has often led him to question his faith: 'There have been moments where it's been a huge test,' he says. 'You read the Bible and life's not simple.' He has sought to be a supportive parent as he affirms and supports and prays often for his daughter Katharine in her struggle with episodes of depression and anxiety. He says that he doesn't pray for his daughter Ellie to be healed of her dyspraxia. He told *The Guardian* (6 July 2018) that he 'has not prayed for his daughter Ellie Welby in relation to her disability because it is part of her and "she is precious".'

Our praise and our quiet confidence are our weapons of spiritual warfare during those hard times.

> And they overcame him by the blood of the Lamb, and by the word of their testimony; and they loved not their lives unto the death.
>
> (Revelation 12.11, KJV)

> You, dear children, are from God and have overcome them, because the one who is in you is greater than the one who is in the world.
>
> (1 John 4.4)

Let's have a closer look at what we mean by overcoming faith and how we can grow into it.

5

Battle stations

One Friday morning I woke up with extreme pain in one eye. It was excruciating. After taking pain killers and using eye wash, the pain continued, so we got into the car and drove to the accident and emergency department of our local hospital. When we eventually got to see a doctor, he said he thought I had conjunctivitis and prescribed some drops. The pain became worse after the drops! Now, my pain threshold is pretty high (childbirth makes a big contribution) but I was suffering so much that I couldn't accept the 'wait and see how it feels tomorrow' option.

We're very blessed to live near one of the country's leading eye hospitals, Manchester Royal, which was our next port of call. Soon, I was sitting face up against an expensive piece of equipment while a senior specialist peered into his side of the scope. He quickly recognized the cause of my pain: an ulcer right at the back of my eye, which could only be spotted by the sophisticated ophthalmoscope. The bad news, he explained, was that this was serious enough to put my sight at risk and would need a course of laser treatment that would start on the following Monday. The good news was twofold: because we had discovered it in the early stages, the chances of any permanent damage were slim (although it was highly likely to leave some scar tissue that would need daily drop treatment for a while, maybe permanently); and, second, the pain could be lessened by some special eye drops – what a relief!

Although I was pleased to have been so brilliantly treated and happy that the pain was under control, I was nevertheless very shaken by the prognosis. Frank and I fumbled through a few prayers once we got home, but neither of us had anything resembling overcoming faith! We called our pastor, Roger, who came over immediately to pray for us. Now, bear in mind that, within our Christian tradition, prayer was conducted in a very British way: calmly, intelligently, sometimes with biblical references, usually in a sitting or kneeling position with heads bowed and voices moderated – which was exactly how this prayer session began. Each of us made a contribution in the usual manner and then there were a few moments of silence while we waited on the Lord. What happened next literally made me jump out of my chair.

Roger leapt to his feet and began to pace animatedly around the room. His voice was raised and his body language resembled that of a cage fighter. He alternated between declarations of the Lordship of Jesus and threats of violence against the enemy (who, incidentally, needed to be reminded that his days were numbered and that he had no authority over this situation). Next, Roger turned to me and began to point fiercely at the affected eye, commanding it to be healed in Jesus' name. Frank, meanwhile, had adopted the foetal position on the sofa and was attempting to rock himself into a state of detachment. Forces of evil were opposed, demons rebuked, curses broken, Christ's victory of sin, sickness and death proclaimed, and gradually a sense of peace filled the room. Roger, looking as if he'd just stepped off a rugby pitch, flopped down into an armchair and we all breathed again.

Frank and I sheepishly asked Roger to explain what had just happened in our lounge. Roger calmly talked us through some Bible verses. Although we had read these verses a number of times, we'd never seen the potential they contained to inspire this kind of spiritual warfare. In fact, to be very transparent about it, both of us were a little sceptical about the style of prayer we'd witnessed. Because we knew Roger well and had observed his godly life, and had followed his teaching and guidance over the years, we decided we must try to open our minds to the reality of this hidden dimension and the possibility of taking part ourselves in the spiritual battle, as and when the Spirit led. This is the most important point – we need the leading of the Holy Spirit. Roger explained that he had received a strong prompting from the Spirit of God to pray in this combative manner; this was not his everyday prayer style but, on occasions, he did go to war in this way when the Lord directed him. His character and witness, combined with the biblical foundation we'd looked at together, made us realize there was a lot more to prayer than we thought.

On Monday we went back to the hospital and a different consultant examined my eye. He kept checking his notes, which I could see contained two large circles representing eyes – one of which was marked with a cross. He asked me to move slightly so that he could use the scope to look into the other eye. A minute or two passed and then he stood up, mumbled something unintelligible and left the room. He returned a few moments later with a colleague, who smiled at me but skipped any pleasantries and picked up the notes. The two men pointed together at the diagram and then the examination of both eyes was repeated by the second doctor, followed by some scratching of heads and furrowing of learned brows. 'Mrs Green,' the first man spoke, 'we can't offer you an explanation but we can tell you there is no evidence of an ulcer on either of your eyes. We wondered whether the doctor you saw may have been mistaken but that's impossible given his notes. How are you feeling? Is the pain still present?' It occurred to me that I had felt hardly any pain over the weekend, which I had put down to the marvellous eye drops, and actually no pain at all since waking up that morning. 'No, I feel fine,' I replied. 'And, by the way, if you need an explanation, I can offer one.' He listened while I gave him the short version, which was simply to recount that we prayed and God had moved a mountain for me. 'Well,' he said, 'that's better than anything we can offer!' We left the doctors wondering what to write on their notes and drove home thanking God for rescuing me without the need for lengthy treatment and eye drops for life. I can still picture us driving along the main highway with an extended arm out of each front window; we looked like a charismatic car!

My faith grew as I saw God perform this healing miracle in my own life. So I believe it's important to share our stories and experiences, because it raises faith in others. There are times, however, when the mountain seems so big that we're not sure we have the faith to see it move. We're also often aware that spiritual warfare is very real. Like the Israelites, we fear that the Goliaths we face, like the Philistine warrior who taunted God's people, seem invincible. How can we be overcomers in the battles we face along the way?

The term 'spiritual warfare' isn't technically a biblical phrase; it doesn't translate specifically from any of the original languages used in Scripture. But it is an accurate description of what the Bible outlines: an invisible realm of reality inhabited by spiritual beings – angels created by God entirely to do his will. Some of these rebelled and now oppose God in many ways, including intervening in earthly activities and, in particular, causing problems for those who try to follow the ways of the Lord. Just the fact that these created beings are invisible to us is enough to allow us to forget (or choose to believe) that they exist at all.

Frank was watching live snooker on TV and I sat down to watch with him. I wouldn't normally stay committed for long to such an expression of wifely duty but I must admit there was something really compelling about this match (I think it was a world championship final and it was very tense and closely fought). It was quite hypnotic to watch the large screen and the assembled Crucible Theatre audience, to listen intently to the hushed observations of the commentators and follow the deeply complex pattern of shots. For a while, I was drawn into the same trance-like condition as my husband.

Suddenly something happened that snapped me back to my senses. A cameraman moved slightly from his out-of-shot position and was immediately visible, cables, headphones and everything. It only lasted a split second and then he was invisible again, but that was enough to remind me that there was more going on than I could see on the screen. Of course, I did know that there were technicians and other crew members moving around out of sight while the big occasion was being broadcast, but I had been lulled into this false sense of feeling that everything I was looking at was all there really was. That's exactly how we can be with this subject of spiritual warfare. We inhabit the land of tangibility. Reality is stuff we can see, touch, hear, smell and taste. Even though we do believe there's more, it's easy to forget. Until something catches us off guard and hits us.

In 2 Corinthians 2.11, Paul confidently declares that we're not unaware of the devil and his evil schemes. We probably need to be a little more aware. I don't mean for one moment that we should go to the opposite extreme; I hate it when people talk about the devil and demons all the time, and everything that goes wrong is ascribed to the forces of darkness. But we do need to remember that, as members of the body of Christ, the Church, we are collectively involved in the cosmic spiritual struggle between the advancing kingdom of God and the rebellious hordes of darkness.

God wants to show us a different approach, however. He has lessons for us from the life of David. David resisted the temptation to wear Saul's armour. He knew that he had known God's strength before against unusual foes; he saw himself as God saw him; David, this young shepherd boy, had killed a bear and a lion. How would he fare against this giant of a man?

We are told how he faced up to Goliath:

> David said to the Philistine, 'You come against me with sword and spear and javelin, but I come against you in the name of the LORD Almighty, the God of the armies of Israel, whom you have defied. This day the LORD will deliver you into my hands . . . All those gathered here will know that it is not by sword or spear that the LORD saves; for the battle is the LORD's, and he will give all of you into our hands.'
>
> As the Philistine moved closer to attack him, David ran quickly towards the battle line to meet him. Reaching into his bag and taking out a stone, he slung it and struck the Philistine on the forehead. The stone sank into his forehead, and he fell face down on the ground.
>
> So David triumphed over the Philistine with a sling and a stone.
>
> (1 Samuel 17.45–50)

God had an unconventional strategy for David. Some might view his strategies for us as unusual. I want to explore three aspects of the journey towards overcoming prayer that may help you. What gives us authority to pray in this way? How does God equip us for the battle? How can we see overcoming prayer worked out in our daily lives?

Overcomers in training

If you follow football you'll often hear of a brilliant young 18-year-old who is rising through the ranks and emerging on to the national stage. But then you discover he's not playing in every match, but may often be a substitute. The trainers and managers are helping him to learn a complete set of skills. They're refining his fitness, seeing whether he has the discipline to eat well, sleep well and orientate his life towards peak fitness training, the right attitude in adversity and the persistent pursuit of new skills.

Like the fledgling footballer, we can often do great things while we are still on the way to having a more complete understanding of overcoming faith in the face of battles.

Overcoming faith will often involve acts of the will, dogged faith and an unwavering belief. But if we only think of it in that heroic way we miss out on the biblical pictures of the athlete in training (1 Corinthians 9.24–25) or the well-organized soldier who ensures he or she has the full protection that they need.

> Finally, be strong in the Lord and in his mighty power. Put on *the full armour of God*, so that you can take your stand against the devil's schemes. For our struggle is not against flesh and blood, but against the rulers, against the authorities, against the powers of this dark world and against the spiritual forces of evil in the heavenly realms. Therefore put on the full armour of God, so that when the day of evil comes, you may be able to stand your ground, and after you have done everything, to stand.
>
> Stand firm then, with the belt of truth buckled around your waist, with the breastplate of righteousness in place, and with your feet fitted with the readiness that comes from the gospel of peace. In addition to all this, take up the shield of faith, with which you can extinguish all the flaming arrows of the evil one. Take the helmet of salvation and the sword of the Spirit, which is the word of God.
>
> And *pray in the Spirit* on all occasions with all kinds of prayers and requests. With this in mind, be alert and always keep on praying for all the Lord's people. (Ephesians 6.10–18)

The armour helps us understand how we are equipped for overcoming. Praying in the Spirit helps us lean on God and not merely trust in our own skills and training. All these things help us understand the nature of spiritual warfare. Warfare is not always about how we attack the enemy of our souls, it is often about how we silence his intimidation and stand our ground. Biblical truths such as we find here are not just for our nurture, but so that we might nurture others, with our prayers being a reflection of all that we believe God desires for his creation and his image bearers.

The belt of truth. There are truths that shape our whole perception of how the world works. The big story of the Bible is the narrative through which we view the whole of life. The big story informs our little story.

The breastplate of righteousness. We need to take hold of the idea that righteousness is a word with strong links to justice, goodness and relational holiness. Our choices, rooted in our beliefs, help shape our attitudes. When we live life through the lens of imitating Jesus because he imitated the Father we are committed to intentional goodness, mercy and grace. Our hearts are protected by the breastplate of righteousness from the insidious corruptions of the enemy. In this way, we're following the King, not worshipping ourselves.

The gospel of peace. As we've noted already, the core Hebrew word related to peace is *shalom*. It has several meanings, which, like a cluster of grapes, derive their strength from a common root. Peace, wholeness, tranquility, welfare, prosperity are just five of them. The soldier in our Ephesians word picture is taking that peace to other places. When we pray, the gospel of peace sets our agenda.

Shield of faith. Because of the story we follow about the love of God expressed in Jesus we have an instinct to have faith. We believe the God of our life histories will be with us wherever we find ourselves under attack or buffeted by difficulty. Sometimes we have to hold up that shield of faith to protect ourselves from the onslaught of our enemies and accusers. Like Shadrach, Meshach and Abednego, we say, 'God will rescue us, but even if he doesn't we will not bow the knee to the idols of this world.'

The helmet of salvation. Someone should write a book about a biblical theology of hats and headgear. We hear about crowns, head coverings and much more. Without diverging from our theme in this chapter, let's remind ourselves that the key insight we need at this moment is that they always carry a symbolic meaning. Imagine that God put a hat on you when you gave your life to him. Imagine that the enemy of your soul sees this and shudders because he knows that the Spirit is at work in you and will be contending for you. Your salvation helmet suggests that you are forgiven, that you have a comforter – the Holy Spirit – and that you are a child of God and a joint heir with Christ (Romans 8.17). Your salvation helmet reminds you of the promises of God expressed in Jesus and the fact that Jesus came to bear your sin, rescued you from death and opened the door to an abundant life (John 10.10).

The sword of the Spirit. The Spirit is at work in us, leading us towards wisdom, discernment and spiritual knowledge. We don't have to have neat, tidy answers to every issue or problem. Sometimes in the middle of our biblical common-sense responses we have to allow for the mystery of how God works in us for others, revealing and reminding us of his truth for that situation.

I'm sure you will agree that this is a very rich picture of what is happening as we put on the whole armour of God.

> For our struggle is not against flesh and blood, but against the rulers, against the authorities, against the powers of this dark world and against the spiritual forces of evil in the heavenly realms.
>
> (Ephesians 6.12)

Pray in the Spirit

With all this armour in place, we're called to 'pray in the Spirit on all occasions with all kinds of prayers and requests' (Ephesians 6.18). This phrase is used elsewhere in the New Testament: 1 Corinthians 14.15 (NIV 1984) says, 'So what shall I do? I will pray with my spirit, but I will also pray with my mind; I will sing with my spirit, but I will also sing with my mind.' Jude 20 (NIV 1984) says, 'But you, dear friends, build yourselves up in your most holy faith and pray in the Holy Spirit.' So, what exactly does it mean to pray in the Spirit?

The Greek word translated 'pray in' can have several different meanings. It can mean 'by means of', 'with the help of', 'in the sphere of' and 'in connection to'. Praying in the Spirit does not refer to the words we are saying. Rather, it refers to how we are praying. Praying in the Spirit is praying according to the Spirit's leading. It is praying for things the Spirit leads us to pray for. Romans 8.26 (NIV 1984) tells us, 'In the same way, the Spirit helps us in our weakness. We do not know what we ought to pray for, but the Spirit Himself intercedes for us with groans that words cannot express.' Sometimes prayer is beyond our intelligent words, we have to pray in the Spirit.

We may speak in another tongue. God knows what is taking place at those moments. But part of what is happening when we pray in this way is communication from God. It can provoke images in our minds that help us understand a situation. We may find that the Spirit reminds us of key Scriptures. A word or a short sentence may form in our minds that will bring understanding of a situation and help us pray. Sometimes others will help us grasp what God is saying in that moment.

Sometimes the revelation is more than symbolic and reflects on current life or history. God is giving us a hint or insight. We may then need to do some research so that we can verify the information about a place or people and pray in an informed way.

There's another lesson this passage teaches us. When I'm in a battle situation, especially if it involves conflict with someone, it can be tempting to become very negative towards them. I can start to feel angry, frustrated, even paranoid about that person and their behaviour. I have to remind myself that my struggle is not against flesh and blood. That changes my perspective altogether!

We all have the potential to do wrong things and to hurt others. When I recognize that about myself it's easier to show grace to others. As I realize that the battle is ultimately with evil spiritual forces it helps me not to carry personal grudges and walk in forgiveness. Yes, the battle is real, but we have an Almighty, victorious God.

From principles to daily discipleship

Recently I was listening to a sermon on the opposition Nehemiah faced (Nehemiah 4), and I was taking notes on my iPhone. Every time I tried to type 'oppo' for opposition the phone offered the predictive text 'opportunity' instead. It got me thinking. For every kind of opposition there's an opportunity. As we've been travelling around the UK delivering community engagement events we've seen this principle in action many times over.

We were on our way to North Devon to run a ROC community conversation. The news came through that we might face some opposition. A group of white witches were opposed to us coming. They were going to protest.

Just for the record, a white witch is defined as 'someone who practises magic for altruistic purposes'. They're often referred to as 'good' or at least 'neutral' but I must admit that we prayed a lot harder than usual on the way there!

The event was taking place at a school. When we arrived it was quite dark. We spent more time than usual praying in the car park. I was asking myself, 'What do white witches look like?' Eventually we had to get out of the car. The event was about to start when a member of the local council turned up. He was quite angry and asking why we had chosen his town. 'My town doesn't need any redeeming,' he told us. We've certainly heard that a few times before. Huge diplomacy is always needed at times like this. A lovely Christian police officer soon came to the rescue. He had the gift of diplomacy and was able to placate the councillor and invite him to take part in the conversation.

The evening went well despite the challenges beforehand. I'm not sure if any white witches came. If they did, no damage was done and the councillor seemed quite happy by the end of it. In the grand scheme of things this wasn't a big battle but the sort that causes a few headaches at the time. We needed to pray, be gracious and diplomatic. Praying grounds you. It can remind you why you are there and who your provider is.

Sometimes the battles are quite major, however. You'll read in Chapter 8 about the miracle provision of a building we were given for our ROC headquarters. I've told the story dozens of times at conferences to encourage others that God provides the resources for the vision! But what I don't speak of as often is the opposition we faced. It all started during our negotiations for the building. We were sharing the possibility with our supporters and prayer team in a newsletter.

A police officer had told me that drugs were a serious issue in the area around The FUSE (the building we were negotiating to buy). We mentioned this in our newsletter to supporters. Somehow the news got out. The phone started to ring continuously with complaints. What gave us the right to say that this community had a drugs problem?

The callers were increasingly irate. I could completely understand where they were coming from. Even though our report was pointing to truth, we wouldn't have wanted to go public in this way! Local social media pages picked up on it and before we knew where we were there were hundreds of unpleasant comments piling up. In fact, although it felt as if the whole town were opposed to us, it was only a vociferous minority, people who preferred to make trouble rather than support the idea of improving their community.

It all got a bit out of control, fuelled by the viral effect of social media. Stress levels were rising. We were aiming to have good relations with the local community, and now things were very strained. In the end, a public meeting was called to hold me to account. The hall was packed out. I was determined not to defend myself, but I wasn't about to give in to calls for me to pull out of the deal. God was opening this door and the enemy was riled. Lots of accusations were levelled at me. I don't think I've ever said sorry as many times in my life, before or since. I was sorry that the factual information we had mentioned had caused offence to local residents. I hadn't intended to give the impression that the whole town was involved in drug-dealing. But I stood firm. We were moving in to help where we could, and local people of goodwill would be invited to partner with us for the good of the community.

We've been in The FUSE for a few years now and things have calmed down but I still remember those early months feeling very nervous and unsure about how this particular mountain would move. Trusting God and persisting in prayer, understanding that the opposition was spiritual rather than personal, and waiting patiently for God's vindication and responding in grace and love – these were the principles that enabled us to overcome this attack.

We need to pray – just to make it through the day

In January 2018 we had a royal visitor at our ROC headquarters. HRH the Princess Royal came to celebrate the fifth anniversary of 'ROC Restore', our restorative justice project. She is Patron of the Restorative Justice Council. I have been reflecting about the visit and lessons learned from the experience. First of all there was the sheer number of things we had to do to prepare!

There was a long list: liaise with the Royal Household to find out requirements; invite people to attend; send save-the-date notices; develop a detailed programme for the visit; submit to a number of security checks; prepare and send invitations; receive replies and prepare badges; design and purchase a plaque; design and purchase certificates; design and purchase signage; determine which staff (and volunteers) were going to do which jobs; clean and prepare The FUSE and the grounds to receive visitors. Then there was a whole mountain of jobs relating to catering, including a special Royal Menu! Plus audio visual stuff (videos, PowerPoints, background music, set lighting, staging, timings, audio and rehearsal). Emergency plans, car parking. Protocol around photos and videos. Briefing, reception and the receiving line to welcome the Princess!

I was invited to be in the receiving line alongside the Lord Lieutenant, Mayor, High Sheriff, one of our Trustees, Sir Peter Fahy, and Rebecca who had developed the project. Normally I'm not lost for words, but when the Princess Royal approached me she asked a question. Up until that point she'd just shaken hands. I suppose it was normal practice on a visit for her to start a conversation with the charity leader. But I struggled to reply and Sir Peter had to step in!

Sometimes we feel like that approaching God. We feel overawed and lost for words. We may even concentrate too much on the proto-col and pomp surrounding our relationship with a holy God.

The Bible says a lot about this:

> Let us then approach God's throne of grace with confidence, so that we may receive mercy and find grace to help us in our time of need.
>
> (Hebrews 4.16)

> Pray in the Spirit on all occasions with all kinds of prayers and re-
> quests. With this in mind, be alert and always keep on praying for
> all the Lord's people. (Ephesians 6.18)

> Pray without ceasing. (1 Thessalonians 5.17, ESV)

But how do you do that? How do you pray without ceasing?

There are seven instructions to be found in Ephesians 6.18.

1 I want you to pray in the spirit.
2 At all times.
3 Pray with all kinds of prayers. In Psalms there is a prayer for every emotion known to humankind. There are complaining prayers. There are crying-out prayers. There are comforting prayers. There are courageous prayers. There are confessing prayers. There are celebrating prayers.
4 Pray about everything you need. Nothing is off limits – health, finances, relationships, work.
5 Always be ready. Spontaneous prayers are great, but prepared prayers are important too. If you have a burden to pray for a place, a people group or a person, do some research so that you can practise informed intercession.
6 Always be ready and never give up. Never stop praying. We may not pray in every waking moment but we want to move from just having a 'praying at set times' mindset to 'praying short prayers throughout the day' habit of mind. Think of it as having a running conversation with God. When something comes up you talk to God about it there and then. Develop this as a habit.
7 And always pray for *all* God's people.

It can be helpful to schedule prayer times throughout the day. Daniel knelt three times a day to pray. The Romans built a forum in every major city, which had a bell tower. The bell would ring six or seven times a day. The Jews and Christians started using these for times of prayer. The Latin word for bell is *cloc* – I like to think that clocks were invented to make time for prayer!

David says, 'Seven times a day I praise you' (Psalm 119.164). Seven times a day may be too challenging for our busy schedules.

How about three times each day like Daniel? You could set an alarm on your phone with a bell chime?

Think about a threefold pattern, such as that given here.

1 Gratitude in the mornings.
2 Intercessions at midday. What matters to you the most? At midday, when stresses of the day are hitting you, remember what matters most. Philippians 4.6–7 reminds us: 'Do not be anxious about anything, but in every situation, by prayer and petition . . .' (See that word 'petition'? Petition means I'm asking God.) 'Do not be anxious about anything, but in every situation, by prayer and petition, with thanksgiving, present your requests to God. And the peace of God, which transcends all understanding, will guard your hearts and your minds in Christ Jesus.'
3 Blessing in the evening. End your day with an encouraging truth. The word 'benediction' means 'a good word'. You'll sleep better because you know God is in control.

Sadly, battle stations are part of the reality of the Christian life, but remember that we are on the side that ultimately wins!

A man had a dream. In the dream he saw a room that had cracks appearing on the walls. He saw someone who looked a bit sinister standing next to a table. The table had rolls of wallpaper. The man was busy covering over the cracks with the wallpaper. As fast as he worked, more cracks were appearing. Nearly all the wallpaper was used. The man couldn't interpret the dream so he went to his pastor. They prayed together. The pastor interpreted the dream. He said that the man in the room was Satan and the room was his kingdom. The cracks appearing on the walls were happening because of all the prayers of the church. The guy who'd had the dream got very excited. He started shouting 'Praise the Lord!' The pastor asked him, 'Why are you so excited'? The man replied, 'There was only one roll of wallpaper left. Satan is running out of wallpaper!'

God wins! Let's remember that when we face battles along the way.

Now we come to moving some community mountains. God has a 'good word' for your community. Let's explore what it is and how to pray about it.

6

Community cohesion

Back in the day, we would sing of our nation being healed or we would ask God to send his salvation to the nation. We often knelt as we cried out to him. Our expectations were expanding.

Not many years previously, however, questions such as these would only be considered relevant in the context of evangelical revivalism, with wholesale personal conversion as the only valid evidence that God was indeed at work. Social transformation was deemed to be a secular goal or, perhaps, the agenda of Christians from the very edges of the liberal wing of the Church who didn't really believe in personal conversion but worked hard to help meet the material needs of their less fortunate neighbours.

Thankfully, there's been something of a wholesale reformation of mission thinking within evangelical churches over the past few decades, thanks largely to great leaders like John Stott and others who have faithfully demonstrated that the Bible contains many examples of God's redemptive purpose for communities. God loves towns, cities, countries, as well as the individuals who inhabit them. His desire for humans is that we live together in harmony and prosperity in the here and now as well as in the life to come.

The abundant life that Jesus came to bring begins with the reversal of the effects of the 'thief' and is usually a gradual process that starts with united, community-focused prayer, which progresses into organized activities that address the social problems of a community: the mountains that need moving.

What many have discovered during these prayer times is that God frequently reveals specific elements of his vision and purpose for a town or city, which are often related to some unique aspects of its latent potential. We experienced exactly this in our home city of Manchester (a community that is notably pioneering, hard-working, creative) and you can read all the details in our book *City-Changing Prayer*, so I'll use different examples in this chapter.

Turning the tide

My friend Lloyd Cooke, a church leader from Stoke-on-Trent in the north-west of England, loves to talk about how God has been starting to restore his city. In 2001, a national survey looking at various socio-economic indicators in 376 towns and cities in England and Wales placed Stoke-on-Trent at the bottom of the list. The unenviable title of 'the worst place to live in the country' proved to be a catalyst for a number of Christian leaders to meet together in order to pray for the area. Some mountain! In a spirit of humility and quiet desperation, the leaders asked God for his divine intervention.

A subsequent city prayer gathering was arranged, during which 2 Chronicles 7.14 was used as a prayer focus ('If my people, who are called by my name, will humble themselves and pray and seek my face and turn from their wicked ways, then I will hear from heaven, and I will forgive their sin and will heal their land'). This proved to be a powerful event as 200 Christians gathered to cry out for God's mercy. Such was the impact of the event that similar united prayer gatherings started to take place each month under the banner of '2C7', attracting several hundred Christians to each meeting.

One of the prophetic messages received suggested that Stoke-on-Trent would be a 'model city'. The leaders were clear that 'model' didn't necessarily mean the biggest or the best but that the city would highlight positive examples of God's work and that other people outside the city might find encouragement from Stoke's example.

Interestingly, over the resultant years there have been a number of 'model' developments, including

- bringing Christian leaders together for regular prayer and fellowship to focus specifically on the needs of the city;
- the use of Faith Action Audits to highlight the community impact of faith-based caring work;

- encouraging positive partnership links between Christian leaders and those in other sectors such as business, local government, education and media;
- organizing an annual civic prayer event;
- setting up a house of prayer to encourage even more regular, city-focused intercession.

What a blessing it is to see leaders have a dream for their city! When prayer turns the tide in a city, town or village, hope starts to be released and a fresh vision for that community starts to emerge from inside and outside the Church. From being the 'worst place to live' in 2001, Stoke was shortlisted for 'UK City of Culture' in 2021. The nomination eventually went to Coventry but this is what the bid materials said:

> We're a proud people, across six towns and one city, built on a history of industrial greatness and we're seeing a resurgence of all things that made this place great. We want to capitalise on the opportunities that UK City of Culture 2021 would bring to the city to propel Stoke-on-Trent forward into greatness, not just through a truly unique arts and culture offer but for the future of the city overall. More quality jobs, better transport connections, opportunities to embrace our entrepreneurial spirit and a city that thrives and grows with its people. A home to be proud of.

The Church in Stoke has followed the prophetic exhortation recorded in Jeremiah 29.7 to seek the prosperity of the place where they live: not just praying for lost people from the comfort of a nice interdenominational worship gathering, but also getting stuck into the real issues of the city and its population; tuning in to the region's unique personality, history and potential to discern the purpose of God and call into being the upturn in fortunes that are in his heart.

Unity in diversity

What can we learn about the personality and purpose of our town or city, and what can the followers of Jesus do to love their community and nurture its potential? How does prayer for that unfold, and can we dare to believe that it might be possible to see the beginning of movement in the mountains of pain, brokenness and despair that characterize districts or whole cities?

I believe the answer lies in the concept of community cohesion. The work we seek to model at Redeeming Our Communities has been recognized in wider civic culture as promoting community cohesion, which is defined like this:

> A cohesive community is one where there is common vision and a sense of belonging. The diversity of people's different backgrounds and circumstances are appreciated and positively valued. Those from different backgrounds have similar opportunities.
>
> (*Improving Opportunity, Strengthening Society*)

The concept was established in the UK following a number of riots and disturbances in 2001. The term had been used in different contexts previously – in Canada, for example. It was also a concept that was felt to help shape understanding of why some communities do not become engulfed in violence. One analysis of 1980s' London, highlighted by *The Guardian*, suggested that the Stonebridge district was spared rioting because of the work of a church-nurtured community centre that promoted hope and connection for thousands every week. The volume of despair was diminished and the sense of belief in the locality amplified because of an intentional desire to suggest another vision for life.

God's call to me from the very beginning of my ministry was to focus prayer on the big, specific issues that were causing social fragmentation, such as lack of aspiration among young people, elderly isolation, family failures, distrust and separation between ethnic groups. These mountains need moving in most of the neighbourhoods of the UK. From the base camp of powerful prayer, the next step was to aim to make communities safer, kinder and stronger by helping integrate people of different backgrounds.

I've often been accused of diluting the gospel because the work we do includes secular groups as well as Christians – the implication is that we should be pointing out the sin in these people's lives, not treating them as equals. What we do is recognize the common goal that is shared by 'people of goodwill' – those who have a vision to improve the lives of their neighbours and are willing to give time, energy, compassion, skill and so on to make a positive difference. Their individual philosophical outlook, personal faith or lack of faith shouldn't be a barrier to cooperation for the common good. In fact, what I've discovered over the years is that this non-judgemental acceptance, this unconditional positive regard of not-yet-Christians can often be the key to developing a relationship that ultimately leads to a faith-sharing opportunity. I've lost count of the number of stories from around the country of people joining Alpha courses after working alongside a Christian for a year or two in a ROC project.

A new commandment?

Our call is to pray for those who don't yet know God and to bless them, not to look down our nose at them or give them leaflets explaining theological concepts. Even those who oppose us are to be prayed for. And this is not just a New Testament concept. Imagine how the exiled Israelites must have felt as they endured life in a pagan city far from home and had to ponder these words of Jeremiah: 'Also, seek the peace and prosperity of the city to which I have carried you into exile. Pray to the LORD for it, because if it prospers, you too will prosper' (Jeremiah 29.7). At the time this was written it was a hard word for them to hear! God knew that they hated those Babylonian idolaters, but here was Jeremiah telling them that God was not bringing them home yet! The idea that they also had to pray for them would have come as a shock.

Their Hebrew mindset was deeply influenced by ideas about the presence of God. As far as they were concerned he dwelt in Jerusalem and desired a people who would live lives of purity in a culture that would nurture that. Why would God keep them there in Babylon, and why would he want to bless a place that did not honour him?

Like the ancient ancestors of our faith, we can fall into the trap of believing that we need to separate ourselves from those who don't honour him. Perhaps we should consider that God honours his people wherever they are and however imperfect that place might be. Jeremiah is one of our first clues that this might be the case.

Jesus' distinctive approach

Jesus believes that the presence of God will be seen at work in people wherever people honour his name. In his signature prayer he sets down a pattern that includes praying that his kingdom will come and that his will might be done on earth as it is in heaven.

He sends out his disciples two by two. When they've been welcomed, eaten with people and prayed for their sick, they're to declare that the kingdom of God has come near to them. The purity status of the hosts is not mentioned, but Jesus tells the disciples to eat what is put in front of them, something that would have not gone down well with the Pharisees who worried about where the food came from, the purity status of household members, the inside and outside of the bowls, and much else.

The tangible presence of God, as opposed to his general presence as the Creator of the universe, finds one expression in the physical presence of those who are in covenant relationship with him. Jesus notes that where two or three gather in his name he is there in the midst of them. He tells the Pharisees, referring to himself, that the kingdom of God is in their midst.

Exclusion or embrace?

As we think about how people understood the presence of God and community structure we should note that two of the groups that were dominant in Jesus' day had strong ideas about the presence of God that led to community division and distance, not community coherence. The Essenes were militant about ritual purity and extended it to every area of life. One of their groups formed a community at Qumran so that they could avoid what they saw as the compromise and corruption of the religious people of Jerusalem. The Pharisees were not as militant, but they demanded the highest standard of purity for Temple worship and saw purity as a custom and way of life in other everyday activities.

Everyday community coherence was not something either group supported. The Pharisees had seven types of person that they considered unclean by virtue of their work (barbers, sheep herders, tax collectors, to name but three). Many of the other cultures of the day had ways of excluding or dehumanizing a person. Roman culture had six levels of male. Slaves, women and children were way down the pecking order.

Jesus modelled something completely different. He touched the impure leper and healed him. He allowed the touch of the woman with an issue of blood and the healing that took place. He saved the woman caught in adultery from death. He ate with the tax collectors and Zacchaeus. God had sent his celebrating angels to marginal shepherds. Jesus allowed a woman to wash his feet with her tears. He welcomed Mary and Martha to learn from his teaching rather than being banished to the other room, as would have been the custom of his day.

He healed the Gentile centurion's servant and restored the wounded ear of one of his captors. He promised paradise to a criminal on a cross. He talked to a Samaritan woman and commissioned her for mission, which to the religious of the day was offensive at four levels at least. He held up Gentiles in the Old Testament as examples of faith and was threatened with death as a result.

Jesus did not retreat from community. He embraced the least, the last and the lost when everybody else was rejecting them. He gave them a chance to experience the love of God because he literally came and dwelt among them. He ate with them, worked with them, talked with them and celebrated the Father with them. They were made in the Father's image and he afforded them dignity and worth as they were, even as he called them to join the kingdom of God and turn from their old ways.

Season and savour

Jesus' rejection of separation and distance is reinforced by his use of the images of salt and light:

> 'You are the salt of the earth. But if the salt loses its saltiness, how can it be made salty again? It is no longer good for anything, except to be thrown out and trampled underfoot.
>
> 'You are the light of the world. A town built on a hill cannot be hidden. Neither do people light a lamp and put it under a bowl.

69

Instead they put it on its stand, and it gives light to everyone in the house. In the same way, let your light shine before others, that they may see your good deeds and glorify your Father in heaven.'

(Matthew 5.13–16)

These are images of presence and proximity. The salt and light preserve and enhance. We need to have a faithful presence if we're to bring about community coherence.

We then start to embody the holiness of God before a watching world. Holiness is a bit of a scary word for many of us. It's often linked to self-examination and fear. But think of it as relational goodness. God wants his image-bearers in the earth to bring his goodness into situations. If we view the Ten Commandments and the book of Proverbs as wisdom for our relationships we then start to ask what brings relational flourishing.

Our activities in our communities start to have a Trinitarian foundation. We love because the Father loves us. We imitate Jesus because he entered our reality. We lean on the Holy Spirit to empower us for relational wisdom so that we might be full of 'love, joy, peace, forbearance, kindness, goodness, faithfulness, gentleness and self-control. Against such things there is no law' (Galatians 5.22–23).

Fruitful outcomes

All this becomes a lived-out word of God when we're present for and engaged with our community. It becomes a contagious holiness. Think about how many testimonies you hear when people say that they knew that there was something different about their friend and they had to find out what it was. People get curious, and then they give you permission to share the Jesus story with them. The fruits of the Spirit noted above become less abstract when you're in the midst of your community juggling your love and annoyance at the same time.

In the midst of all this activity we pray. We pray to ask God to honour the promise of his character, which is implicit in asking in his name. We pray to open up the conversation with God where he can prompt us to think and act. We pray to remind each other of truth. We pray that God might prosper the place where we are. We

pray that he'll bring his shalom, his peace, and the community healing that will follow.

I was very privileged and totally surprised to receive an OBE
(Order of the British Empire) in 2012 for services to 'community
cohesion'. I'm grateful to my pastor, Anthony Delaney, for secretly
nominating me, and for the endorsement of Sir Peter Fahy, who was
the Chief Constable of Greater Manchester Police at the time. I found
out since that the way the process works is that, following a nomination, a team of people will research your suitability to receive the
award. At that point in the history of ROC we'd launched about 60
community projects aimed at addressing issues such as youth antisocial behaviour, through after-school clubs and other activities. As
a direct result of these, recorded incidents of ASB (anti-social behaviour) and crime fell significantly. The police and local authorities
were impressed. Her Majesty the Queen was unwell on the day of the
awards ceremony so Prince Charles presented me with my medal. 'I
believe you've been reducing crime,' he said as he pinned the ribbon
on my dress. I wanted to explain that it was all down to the power
of prayer, but as I opened my mouth to reply the steward nearby was
ushering the next recipient on to the podium!

Insurmountable?

I'd been travelling back and forth to Northern Ireland for a number
of years and always saw huge potential for what ROC could offer
there. Then an interesting thing happened that took our engagement there up a gear. I'd got to know Sir Matt Baggott when he was
Chief Constable in Leicester and we launched ROC at the NEC in
Birmingham (more on this in Chapter 10). A few years later, in 2009,
he was appointed Chief of the Police Service of Northern Ireland
(PSNI). Matt asked us to launch ROC in Northern Ireland and we
started planning towards it. However, quite a few people said it
couldn't be done. The idea of communities working together and
churches working together was a massive challenge. The historical feud between the communities that identified as Catholic or
Protestant was well known. It was not a mere war of words, and relationships were often hindered by the memory of violence and death

on local streets. There was also real hostility towards the police in some sections of both communities.

We prayed and were reminded again that nothing is too difficult for God. There were more problems to tackle than we could ever have imagined, but nevertheless we successfully launched ROC at the Waterfront Arena in Belfast in May 2012. Over 1,500 people came together from a variety of backgrounds, and the sense of strong togetherness was tangible. One of the highlights was seeing people from very diverse backgrounds sharing a platform, including the Chief Constable of the PSNI alongside Martina Anderson. Martina had spent 13 years in prison because of her activities in the Provisional IRA. This was not a platform party that many would have predicted.

Hope is contagious. What we model in one city can inspire other cities with hope and provide practical, proven resources. If our dream is merely a sentimental belief that things would be better if we were all a bit nicer, then it's unlikely to capture minds and become embedded in the patterns of our thinking.

Since the launch at the Waterfront Arena we've seen a number of projects emerge that address community needs. This started with the ROC Café after-school youth groups in different parts of Belfast.

The work continued to develop and we took the step of employing a full-time coordinator, Keeva Watson. She's passionate about communities and studied community development at university. Keeva was able to use her expertise to support the youth work. But she also has a real heart for older people and has developed an award-winning befriending scheme in Rathcoole in partnership with a Methodist church

More recently, we had an unprecedented opportunity to work alongside the Department for Justice to deliver two ROC Conversation community engagement events in east Belfast.

The next few years look even more exciting as we undertake the challenge to deliver work in areas of low community capacity. The incredible thing is that ROC is being recognized as a key partner in tackling paramilitary activity among young people. The BBC recently produced a documentary called *Shot by My Neighbour*, which features the area in Belfast where we will be running some community conversations. It is a real privilege to be undertaking this work with some local churches in the area who have been faithfully serving the community, despite the difficult circumstances.

Walking humbly towards the possibility of a redeemed community

A short time ago we were running some community engagement events in east Belfast. The harrowing news items that you hear about the Northern Irish troubles often feature this tough area.

I was a bit nervous about the trip, although I have been travelling back and forth to Northern Ireland for more than fifteen years. It's clear that, despite the peace agreement that is in place, the legacy of war lives on. The peace walls still literally separate the Protestant and Catholic communities.

It was brilliant to prayer walk around the neighbourhood with people who knew the history. We went to see the new C. S. Lewis Square. The writer Clive Staples Lewis – known the world over as C. S. Lewis – was from east Belfast. The legendary footballer George Best was one of east Belfast's most popular sons. Born on 22 May 1946, the Manchester United and Northern Ireland star – considered the best player in the world by Pele – was brought up on the Cregagh estate and can be seen on some of the many murals that you find there. (He died in November 2005.) Harland & Wolff's iconic yellow cranes, Samson and Goliath, dominate the view across the east of the city. Built by German firm Krupp, they were installed in 1969 and 1974 respectively. They are the city's most identifiable pieces of industrial heritage.

As you walk and pray, you start to feel, see and hear the culture and spirit of the city

The following evening we were in the Lower Shankill area. The Shankill Road (from Irish, *Seanchill*, meaning 'old church') is a road in a militant Protestant enclave in west Belfast. Walking around the area I was particularly struck by the new murals. Belfast city council's Re-imaging Communities programme replaces old murals with new ones, charting the social, cultural and industrial heritage of the Lower Shankill area.

As part of Community Relations and Cultural Awareness Week 2015, artworks were created to reflect local issues and 'create a *lasting vision* of good relations'. The art works are part of a long-term Housing Executive plan 'to help local communities remove the outward symbols of sectarianism through the medium of art'.

Artist Lesley Cherry, from Shankill Estate Artworks, said she believes in 'using art as a catalyst for change, be that commenting on social issues, housing, employment or civil rights'. She added: 'The residents of the Shankill estate are also aware of how this approach can change attitudes not only within their own community, but to others who visit their community; *how they are perceived* and how they want to be perceived.'

In the midst of it all you ask yourself what role you might have in this complex web of history, religion and personal sorrow. They told me that because I was an outsider that would help. They told me that I would not be wrapped up in the mindset or spirit of the place. They suggested that I would see the solution not the problem. We then brought people together to seek very specific outcomes.

Sometimes a situation will need fresh people. Sometimes it just needs fresh eyes.

7

Prophetic prayer

I was teaching a group of students about the spiritual gift of prophecy at The Message Trust Academy. As part of the class we always prayed for the students. We came to a young man called Sam. Suddenly I heard God say that Sam was a poet and that he would write a book of poetry. As I started to speak that out I was aware of how specific it was. It's either right or wrong! Now, with sharing a word like this you occasionally hear feedback immediately from the person who is receiving the word. But often you may not hear back for some time or even at all, especially when it's a large group of people and there are multiple words shared. I can't count the number of times I've been at a conference or visiting a place when someone approaches me about a word I shared with them years before that has now come to pass.

With Sam, it was the next day. He was a shy guy and I couldn't gauge anything at the time the word was shared. But the next day I saw him and asked him. He said he'd been a bit freaked out. He told me that he'd been writing poems since childhood. He'd never shown anyone his poetry. They were all kept in a box in a secret place. He also told me that his grandmother was a poet with books published!

The impact of sharing this word with Sam was the confidence it released in him to explore and use his gift. The word releases faith. He now felt he could share his work. He now knew God had a plan for his life. He knew his talent was from God.

We were exploring how the spiritual gift of prophecy is given by God to build up the Church (1 Corinthians 14.1–5). How does the gift of prophecy intersect with our prayers? How does it help us build a mountain-moving prayer mindset? How do we hear from God? When God speaks, how do I work out what to do next?

Prayer is not just speaking to God; it's also hearing from God

People are meant to live in an ongoing conversation with God, speaking and being spoken to.   (Willard, *Hearing God*)

Prophetic prayer happens when, while praying, we receive revelation from the Holy Spirit. It's the Holy Spirit sharing knowledge that we would have no way of knowing by our human ability alone. The difference between straight prophecy and prophetic prayer has to do with the direction of the prophetic word. Straight prophecy is the Lord's declaration to a person or group of people. Prophetic prayer is aimed towards God in the form of praying for his purposes and plans to come to fruition. John 17.21 is an example of a prophetic prayer. In it, Jesus prophetically prayed, instructed and decreed the Father's will concerning himself, his disciples and the Church: 'that they may all be one, just as you, Father, are in me, and I in you, that they also may be one in us, so that the world may believe that you have sent me' (John 17.21, ESV).

As part of the course that Sam was on, we would pray for each student and ask God to speak prophetically. This was always my favourite part of our times together. But it was also a little bit scary. People who have a prophetic gift sometimes feel the pressure of people's expectations at times like this. I always remember Gerald Coates, one of the UK's leading pioneers in the renewal movement of the past 30 years, saying, 'A prophet can only bring what they hear God say. If we don't hear anything we have nothing to bring!'

Weighing and testing

Our gifts from God have to work in partnership with some of the fruits from the same Holy Spirit. I always teach that prophetic words should be delivered with humility and with the idea of testing in mind. For example, I'll often use phrases such as, 'I believe God is saying', rather than 'God says', which is very different. Promptings from God can also be expressed as questions: if God tells you there's an adultery issue, ask whether there are problems in the marriage. Prophecy is often for the whole congregation or gathering to hear, but some insights, like the one above, should be shared privately and with wisdom and dignity, so that our kindness can be part of the restoration God may have for a broken life.

In our humanity we'll sometimes say things that didn't come from God but from our own enthusiasm or fleshly biases. If we're careful in how we express prophetic insight it can help people believe in the gifts of God as we come in humility and with sensitivity. That there will sometimes be mistakes is clear from the biblical record. Paul encourages us: 'Two or three prophets should speak, and the others should weigh carefully what is said' (1 Corinthians 14.29). We weigh the prophetic utterance against what the Bible tells us of the character of God. We consider whether it reflects how it fits with patterns of scriptural truth. If it has a predictive quality we ask how it might shape our thinking and we await the unfolding in due course. With that proper caution in mind, let us now try and take hold of the truths that God has for us with respect to hearing from him and praying in the light of that revelation.

Jesus promises that we will recognize his voice: 'My sheep listen to my voice; I know them, and they follow me. I give them eternal life, and they shall never perish; no one will snatch them out of my hand' (John 10.27–28).

Studies have shown that sheep can recognize the unique sing-song voice tones of their shepherd. They will not respond to another voice in the same way. When we're listening for the voice of God, so eloquently expressed in Jesus, we will reflect on the character of God and biblical patterns to help us weigh what we believe we're hearing. Our faith then increases when we become more and more aware that we're hearing from God.

What is God saying to you?

God may choose any one of many different ways to communicate to you, according to what's best at particular times and in particular circumstances. You may sometimes hear God's message in dramatic ways, such as through angels, visions, dreams or miraculous events.

But more often, you'll hear God speaking through your thoughts, and he'll use ordinary practices, such as reading the Bible, praying quietly, learning from circumstances or seeking counsel from other Christians, to reach out to you as you think about them.

God will use dramatic means to get your attention when necessary, but his goal is for you to be so closely connected to him that you'll pay attention whenever he speaks to you. Usually, God speaks through what people have described as a 'still, small voice' to encourage those he loves to choose to keep walking closely with him through life.

Hearing from God is an important part of the prayer journey. It can often start by simply saying to the Lord, 'Please speak to me, I'm listening.' The gift is developed over time, as with all the spiritual gifts. Time spent in prayer increases and shapes the gift. Spending time with prophetic people has been really key for me. As it says in Proverbs 27.17, 'iron sharpens iron'.

How do we listen to God?

Let's have a look at how we can hear from God in the ways we have just described. Dave, my co-author, describes some of his own experiences.

Thoughts. One day, as a man walked towards me to receive prayer, I felt God say there was an issue with a popular theology at the time which had become a burden to him. That helped the conversation and the prayer that followed.

Pictures. Praying one day for a man who worked in a cassette duplication firm, I shared a picture of a tape that had become very tangled but could be restored if wound in slowly. He understood this picture and how it might help him grow as a believer.

Dreams. Read on for a story about a dreaming vicar and his words of encouragement for the ROC team.

Daydreaming. This often happens when you're thinking about something and you start to imagine how it might be. People see things in their mind's eye well before those things come to pass. I imagined 600 people at a children's ministry conference – 2,000 turned up and the event went on to touch over 20 nations in the years that followed.

Impressions. This can often be one word. I frequently experience this as an insight into the gifting that someone has and that could be nurtured in them. For a long time I thought maybe it was just me being observant, but one day I got the impression that a man I was having a conversation with had a prophetic word for me. I told him, he prophesied and one of the things he said related to my impressions and how I needed to be aware that some of them were from God and had to be acted on.

Revelation from Scripture. Sometimes a phrase or word captures you. You start to connect it with what you already know. The Holy Spirit's work is often in the application of that to your life or the ministry of your church in the neighbourhood. You are starting to get prophetic insight for your situation and can pray in the light of that.

There are traditions of Bible reading that actively encourage this. You read a passage slowly twice and then stay with a verse or phrase that has particularly spoken to you. This slow reading can be an important doorway to prophetic insight.

Discernment. This is closely related to impressions and can relate to personal issues someone may face. But they can also relate to the spiritual history of a place. I heard a story of a person recently who would often ask people how they were feeling when he was preparing to pray for them. If their response reflected emotions close to the problem he was discerning he would pray clearly and calmly for their release from that bondage.

Discernment of places pushes us towards research. What has the place or building been used for in the past? What pain or brokenness has there been there in the past? How might that still touch the present-day conduct of people in that place? How will the shalom of God change or, in the case of good history, multiply that?

Revelation

At the heart of all these ways we hear from God is the idea of a revelation. This is not new knowledge about God beyond what we know from the Bible. It is about the application of eternal truths to today and a deeper understanding on our part of who God is, who we are and what the role of the Church is in the world today.

Faith grows from that revelation; faith that moves mountains.

Faith that moves mountains has had a redemptive revelation about what God desires to do.

Where there is no vision [no redemptive revelation of God], the people perish; but he who keeps the law [of God, which includes that of man] – blessed (happy, fortunate, and enviable) is he.

(Proverbs 29.18, AMPC)

When we began ROC we were responding to a vision for our city that we were absolutely certain had been revealed to us by God. Manchester, like many of our cities and towns, was full of perishing people. Problems, challenges and tragedies were reported daily in our news bulletins. Crime was running high – particularly violent crime. Businesses were struggling; homelessness was rising; young people especially were at risk of choosing pathways to adulthood that would lead them into difficulties and away from wholesome opportunities. God revealed to us his own desire for our city, which was to reverse these negative trends and bring transformation. Some of our group wanted to pray against what they perceived as dominating spiritual powers over the city, but after waiting on God in the Spirit we all began to sense that his redemptive revelation was strongly positive. He revealed to us the latent potential contained in our city and called us to call it into being. We were to speak out the redemptive revelation.

In the same way that a parent speaks out the positive elements in the personality of her child in order to fan them into flame, so we were believing that a change in our city was possible. We were looking upon our city as a place that God wanted to bless, when it might have been tempting to look upon it as lost and in need of judgement. We were praying for the wisdom of God to start to prevail there.

We were hearing from God about the good news of Jesus and believing for things not yet seen, all at the same time.

So faith comes from hearing, that is, hearing the Good News about Christ. (Romans 10.17, NLT)

Now faith is the substance of things hoped for, the evidence of things not seen. (Hebrews 11.1, KJV)

This revelation often has a dream-like – or daydream-like – quality and comes about when the Holy Spirit connects our belief in the character of God and the work of Jesus with our current reality. God uses every part of us in those moments as our minds, emotions and his heart combine to imagine a better future and the emergence of his kingdom. This in turn informs our prayer, our thinking and our actions.

How is your faithometer?

Faith is like a seed that is planted in your heart and your mind. At the appointed time God will give you a harvest of what you need. For this seed to germinate and grow, the roots of our whole lives need to be deep already: 'Let your roots grow down into him, and let your lives be built on him. Then your faith will grow strong in the truth you were taught, and you will overflow with thankfulness' (Colossians 2.7, NLT).

As you start to receive prophetic revelation about the future plans of God and his desire for your neighbourhood, your seemingly small seeds of faith can produce a large harvest:

'The Kingdom of heaven is like a mustard seed, which a man took and planted in his field. Though it is the smallest of all seeds, yet when it grows, it is the largest of garden plants and becomes a tree, so that the birds come and perch in its branches.'

(Matthew 13.31–32)

'A farmer went out to sow his seed. As he was scattering the seed, some fell along the path, and the birds came and ate it up. Some fell on rocky places, where it did not have much soil. It sprang up quickly, because the soil was shallow. But when the sun came up, the plants were scorched, and they withered because they had no root. Other seed fell among thorns, which grew up and choked the plants. Still other seed fell on good soil, where it produced a crop—a hundred, sixty or thirty times what was sown.'   (Matthew 13.3–8)

There's a lot we can learn from people of faith in history. It's also good to celebrate what God has done before in our own lives. Here is an example.

George Müller, (born 27 September 1805; died 10 March 1898) was a Christian evangelist and the director of the Ashley Down orphanage in Bristol, England. He cared for 10,024 orphans during his lifetime and provided educational opportunities for the orphans to the point that he was even accused by some of raising the poor above their natural station in British life. He established 117 schools, which offered Christian education to more than 120,000 children, many of whom were orphans.

One morning, all the plates and cups and bowls on the table were empty. There was no food in the larder and no money to buy food. The children were standing, waiting for their morning meal, when Müller said, 'Children, you know we must be in time for school.' Then lifting up his hands he prayed, 'Dear Father, we thank Thee for what Thou art going to give us to eat.'

There was a knock at the door. The baker stood there, and said, 'Mr Müller, I couldn't sleep last night. Somehow I felt you didn't have bread for breakfast, and the Lord wanted me to send you some. So I got up at 2 a.m. and baked some fresh bread, and have brought it.'

Mr Müller thanked the baker, and no sooner had he left when there was a second knock at the door. It was the milkman. He announced that his milk cart had broken down right in front of the orphanage, and he would like to give the children his cans of fresh milk so he could empty his wagon and repair it.

Faith gives birth to an expectation that God will answer. Hearing from God is a key part of this process.

God speaks to us in many different ways, on all kinds of occasions, about a whole variety of things. We spent time as a team in early 2017 praying about our finances, a regular occurrence for charities like ours. We needed an urgent breakthrough in a short period of time and for a significant sum. No pressure!

So we increased our praying. In January 2017, I was due to speak at a Baptist church in Nottingham. My prayer partner, Wendy, and I travelled together. We always use road trips as an opportunity to pray. At some point on that journey Wendy received the word 'snowdrops' as we were praying about a financial breakthrough. Snowdrops are described in horticultural literature as a welcome assurance that the brighter days of spring are on their way. They are a striking bloom in the winter months when little else is growing. Snowdrops flower between January and March. We spent some time praying about the word and believed God was saying very clearly that we would see a breakthrough in finances before the end of March.

We arrived in Nottingham and had a good morning with the church. I remember sharing with the church a little bit about ROC and our partnership with the police. At the end of the service I was approached by a young man called Chris. He was a police officer and had been encouraged by my message. I found out later from Simon, the church leader, that it was Chris's first time in church. His wife had invited him because she knew about our work with the police and hoped he would find it relevant. Simon told me that Chris had given his life to the Lord at the end of the service.

As we left church that morning, on a high, we decided to visit Kelham Hall in Newark, as it was nearby, and the venue for the imminent ROC Conversation that was coming up in March. As we arrived at Kelham Hall we were greeted at the entrance with a field entirely covered with snowdrops. It was the only sighting of snowdrops during the trip.

Once back at the office I shared with the whole team about how God had spoken. I said that I believed we would see a financial breakthrough by 31 March. Money started to flow in in dribs and drabs throughout January and February. But by 31 March we were still £20,000 short of our target. Wendy and I were feeling nervous. Why had we said 31 March so categorically? That evening, Frank and I had dinner with a good friend. She had been praying for us but was not aware of the urgent need for funds. At the end of the meal, around 9 p.m. on 31 March, she said she felt led by God to donate £20,000.

I expect many of us have experienced that kind of 'last minute' answer to prayer! Yes, it stretches your faith, and that can be hard to bear, but I wouldn't swap any of those experiences as they've taught me the most about trusting in God and what he has spoken prophetically.

In the next chapter we'll explore how prayer can lead to divine favour. Extraordinary things can happen when we pray and step into God's will for our lives. Over three years we consistently prayed for a new building for our ROC headquarters. During that time we heard God speak very clearly through a number of prophetic words. One came from a local vicar who receives prophetic dreams. Here's an excerpt from Nick's written message to me:

> In my dream I was taken on a tour of a new building. It was very beautiful and was constructed from a lot of glass. Inside there were people having coffee and the atmosphere was very warm and hospitable. You were proudly showing me around.
>
> Now, I don't want to offer my interpretation of all this. But the following things struck me.
>
> 1 new building
> 2 light, glass, place of 'the son'
> 3 location – perhaps surprising.
>
> Also, it seemed to be about Ivy Church. [I, Debra, was delighted, as this is my church!] I should perhaps have sent this to the Church Team Leader, Anthony, but it was you that I was talking to and so I've learnt over the years to direct these things to the person I'm speaking to, not the things it's about.
>
> You may do with this as you wish. Love, Nick.

Bear in mind that Nick didn't know that we were even looking for a building! It was very timely confirmation and a great encouragement. But we still had to wait. And the reference to Ivy Church was interesting. I didn't understand it at the time, but a couple of years later Ivy Church planted a congregation in the building we were given, Ivy FUSE church!

I love the fact that some people hear so clearly from God in dreams and visions! The prophet Joel tells us that God has a promise for us:

> I will pour out my Spirit on all people.
> Your sons and daughters will prophesy,
> your old men will dream dreams,
> your young men will see visions.
>
> (Joel 2.28)

Nick's dream came as a huge encouragement to me because it confirmed some of the words we'd received in our regular prayer meetings. He also had an amazing track record! I could tell you about another dream he shared with me relating to the national launch of ROC at the NEC in Birmingham, which proved to be very accurate. To those of you who hear from God through dreams, dream on!

Let me tell you more about a big dream we had for a place to develop the work of Redeeming Our Communities, the mountain-moving faith it needed and how the favour of God came to be shown to us.

8

Divine favour

One of my African friends used to poke fun at my Britishness – 'Your God is too small!' he'd say, often in the context of a meeting to plan an event. A group of us were meeting to pray and I thought I was believing big; we'd booked the Manchester Velodrome for a prayer gathering; he said we should have booked Old Trafford or Maine Road and exercised African-style faith. He was pulling my leg – in fact he was genuinely impressed that my vision had stretched to this extent.

The capacity of the Velodrome was ten times that of the biggest place we'd used before, and the resources we were going to need to make this event a success were far greater than we could humanly muster. We began to pray, and the banter was replaced with urgent petitions about the magnitude of the proposed occasion. My friend moved into prophetic mode and began to declare that God was pleased with our plans and would certainly provide everything we needed; sufficient funds would be available to us, musicians, equipment, publicity, volunteers to serve as stewards, support from civic leaders, and so on. 'Provision', he declared, follows vision.'

I really love that statement. Over the years I've seen the truth of it in many ways as God has miraculously answered prayers for people I know, and in the past few years it's become so real in my own life that it's now a part of the DNA of ROC. We never begin a project with everything we need, but we do always begin with vision. We've learned to trust God to provide because he always has. But here's the thing: sometimes your vision needs work. Maybe your God isn't African enough! Thankfully, the Lord helps us clarify things when we wait for him in prayer and watch and listen for his guidance, which often comes through prophetic words that cause us to raise our expectations. Sometimes we can be happy to settle for a hill when God wants to push us towards us a mountain!

Back in 2012, our ROC HQ was a small office in the corner of Lancaster House, the home of The Message Trust in Sharston, Manchester. Our good friend Andy Hawthorne kindly provided the space for us free of charge. It was such a support in the early years of ROC, but we were running out of space. As our influence around the country increased, our team was growing fast and we really needed a bigger home. We started to dream of having our own head-quarters. It wasn't just a nice idea; we urgently needed a place where we could train volunteers, host conferences, run events and projects. So we set about doing two things. First, we turned the dream into a vision – a specific, defined thing: we 'saw' in our mind's eye a large detached building with its own outdoor space and car park, as well as a number of offices. It had other rooms for training sessions and larger gatherings, maybe a suitable space for a conference or even a church plant. Then we turned to prayer. Just days later I got the email from Nick whom I referred to in the previous chapter. I shared it with our team, and our excitement levels increased!

It's easy, when writing about things years later, to forget about the frustrations and disappointments that challenge us when we're praying to move mountains. An uplifting prayer time with prophetic words and faith-building Scripture references can often be followed by weeks of silence and spiritual dryness. The problems and oppor-tunities of everyday normality can erode our confidence in God, and I don't want to give the impression that I was immune to this kind of thing. I frequently found myself mentally compromising the vision in the face of our urgent need for more space. Maybe we should be seeking a stop-gap solution, a temporary home that would be a step-ping stone to the full realization of God's provision. At my lowest points I even felt as though I was completely off target; after all, if we did find a perfect new building, how would we ever be able to fund the extra costs? There'd be rent, rates, insurances, utilities, mainten-ance and so on, not to mention the need for extra staff. Did I really want to be woken up in the middle of the night to be told about a break-in or a fire?

Thankfully, my team helped me stay focused. We downed tools

twice a week to spend quality time praying, so my dark days didn't survive long enough to knock me out completely. After a few months, we were offered what we thought might be an opportunity. Despite not ticking all the boxes, it was owned by a Christian and the rent was going to be realistic, although we'd have to take a big step of faith to pay any rent at all after benefiting from The Message's generosity for the past few years. I had been asking myself whether our dream/vision might have been a little too 'African', so I went along to view it with a little tinge of excitement.

It was a suite of offices above a chip shop in Cheadle Hulme. As I climbed the slightly dangerous, outdoor wooden steps at the rear of the block of shops, my enthusiasm took a dive. Inside was drab and unpleasant; it really wasn't that much bigger than our current office, and had nothing like enough space to hold any training sessions, let alone a conference. The thought of all our clothes smelling of chip fat was enough to close the door, and I left feeling disappointed but relieved. I was more determined than ever not to settle for second best but to press on to find what God had shown us.

Next up was Elm House in Withington, a former health centre. They wanted £225,000 to buy it and we had no money. More prayer needed. A few days later, quite out of the blue, I received a call from a Christian couple. They'd heard about it and were considering making a large donation. They were going to pray about it and let me know in a day or two. How exciting! This must be it! They called the next day to say it didn't feel right. Intriguingly, though, they added that they believed God had told them he had something far better for us. Not what you want to hear at that point, but we tried our best to believe it and went back to prayer.

In one of our prayer meetings, we refocused on Nick's dream and, in particular, the glass-fronted building he so clearly 'saw'. My good friend Wendy, who regularly hears from God in specific ways, suggested that perhaps the building we should be praying for was a well-known landmark just off the M60 motorway in Stockport. It's a huge, pyramid-shaped structure completely surrounded in glass and visible for miles around. If it hadn't been Wendy's suggestion I think we all would have just laughed it off but, given her track record of accurate prophetic prayers, we decided instead not just to pray but also to go and investigate. The building had been empty for a few years during the economic downturn in the 1990s when the developer went into liquidation. The Co-op Bank had repossessed it and was now using part of it as a call centre. We drove the three or four miles full of faith and expectancy. Maybe the time had come! Could this be the moved mountain we'd prayed so hard for?

We boldly ignored the sign saying that all visitors would need an appointment and marched up to the reception desk. More divine favour enabled us not only to get past the entrance barriers but also to be given a guided tour of the empty floors. Like mighty warriors, we claimed every place we laid our feet, and drove victoriously back to base. Surely it would just be a matter of time before the phone would ring and the CEO of the Co-op Bank would be inviting us over for lunch. We were greatly encouraged when Frank told us that he had a friend who knew one of the senior directors of the Co-op Bank. He was going to set up a meeting for us to present our community work to the Board and was confident that they would be keen to help us – especially as they have a strong community focus themselves and deep roots in the north-west of England. They would almost certainly want to let us have some of the unused space in their prestigious HQ and probably be keen to sponsor our work across the country. The whole thing seemed to bear the stamp of God's approval.

However, the days went by and turned into weeks. Frank and his friend did get to meet the director, but not the Board. The bank was going through some very troubled waters and was facing big challenges throughout the business, including the need to sell a lot of its property and close many branches. The idea of supporting a charity in any tangible way wasn't going to appear on any agenda for the foreseeable future.

The moral of this little story is that sometimes we can overestimate our spiritual gifts. It's humbling to be reminded that the treasure we have is housed in vessels of clay. Our fleshly fervour can resemble spirituality quite readily and we need to be careful not to get carried away in our desire to see God's promises fulfilled. Disappointed? Yes, we were. Discouraged? Yes, we were. Determined to hang in and continue to trust the Lord? Yes, we were.

But to look at it from another angle, if the faith we need in order to see a mountain moved is like a mustard seed then that means it doesn't have to be impressive in and of itself. It's organic and full of potential. If it finds the right conditions and is properly nurtured, it will grow and eventually become highly visible and very fruitful. Further, we know that God often closes doors that appear to be ideal opportunities because there are even better ones just around the corner.

After a few more months we went to see a warehouse near Wythenshawe hospital. It had been previously used by the Lighthouse Church and was much bigger than the other buildings we'd seen. The sense of anticipation stirred once more as Frank and I went to have a look around. There was plenty of space and loads of potential, but it would need a lot of cash to make it work. Undaunted, we reported back to the team and got stuck into prayer again. The short version is that this just dragged on and in the end fizzled out. God had closed another door.

More months went by and our little open-plan office felt smaller than ever. I was having a bit of a grumble about it when the phone rang. It was the Cabinet Office! Somehow the Government had heard that we were looking for a new HQ and it just so happened that the Department for Education had an empty building in Partington, not far from the Trafford Centre, which might be available. Would I be interested in having a look at it? My heart leapt, and before I could think about a balanced response I was agreeing a date for a visit.

Now, Frank and I are very different. I'm a glass-half-full person – I always see the positives about things even though there may be challenges and problems. Frank, on the other hand, has been described (unfairly, but only just) as a glass-half-smashed person! You can imagine the discussion we had when I described The FUSE to him. It's a purpose-built, state-of-the-art community centre that cost £5.5 million. Constructed in 2011, it had been run by a small, local charity for a year or so but had to close due to lack of funds. It didn't take Frank long to do some ball-park calculations – overheads would cost roughly £100,000 per annum. Where would we get that from? On top of that, we'd need a caretaker, cleaning staff, a receptionist and maybe more staff – unless we could persuade our current team to add some new tasks to their HQ roles. He was adamant that we couldn't even consider it and I would have to view it on my own.

I went along to see it in December 2013. The first thing I noticed was the large logo on the outside of the glass-fronted building: 'The FUSE', spelt out in four strong colours that were exactly the same as the colours in our ROC logo. Spine tingling! I drove into the large car park and noted plenty of outdoor space, including a floodlit, weather-proof artificial five-a-side pitch. Next door is a secondary school and one of the staff there had the FUSE keys. As we entered the main reception area my eyes were drawn to the 30-foot high ceiling, which makes the space seem vast and airy. It was furnished like a large café and those four ROC colours were repeated in the decor and in the signs pointing to Auditorium, Dance Studio, Sports Hall, Green Room, Art Workshop, Conference Room and Kitchen. I was speech-less! Upstairs were fully furnished offices with computers, copiers and cupboards. Everything looked brand new. Each room had a large, quirky clock fixed to the wall, made up of individual numbers set in an avant-garde non-circle – I expect you can guess the colours of the numbers!

It just seemed so huge. Way bigger than anything we could have imagined even at the height of enthusiastic prayer team gatherings! I wandered around the building in a bit of a daze. Even though it had been closed down for a year it was in amazing condition. We looked around the 300-seat theatre with its electrically operated lighting hoists, fully equipped sound system and enormous cinema screen. The retractable bank of fold-down cinema seats made it ideal as a space for a conference or church meeting.

I suppose I knew immediately that it was the provision God was making for us. Every box was ticked. But could we really make it work? First we had to put together a business plan to show how we could pay the bills. And would the Government really hand it over to us when other groups had been turned away? We would need the favour of God, that's for sure.

One of my biggest challenges was persuading Frank to get on board. He was right to ask how on earth we could increase our income by such a large amount, and hit the ground running as bills would be coming in from day one. He did at least agree to come and have a look around, and we booked a second trip. I'll never forget the look on his face as we stepped into the atrium. His eyes moved immediately up, exactly as mine had, to take in the cavernous space. He turned to me and said, 'This is the favour of God – we must do whatever it takes.' As we walked around, he kept on pointing out the colour scheme (as though I hadn't told him all about it beforehand!). 'These are our colours, everywhere you look! And have you seen the clocks?' Mr Glass-half-smashed was suddenly full of faith! No need for any deliberations – God was flinging wide the door; all we had to do was demonstrate our ability to make a success of running The FUSE, which meant not only paying the bills but also enabling it to function as a community asset.

Negotiations took six or seven months, during which time our prayers moved up a gear to address the practical challenges. We appealed to our faithful supporters for a £50,000 fighting fund to enable us to cover costs during our setting-up phase. We set a date by which we needed this before we would sign the lease. One week before the date, the fund hit £60,000. Hallelujah!

We were offered the building on a 22-year rent-free lease. Yes, I had to pinch myself. The other questions were still unanswered, but we knew it was right. We signed the lease. On 29 July 2014 we moved into The FUSE. It is our amazing miracle provision. Everyone agreed. We felt as though we were experiencing the unprecedented favour of God! Guess what we did as soon as we moved in? We held a celebratory prayer meeting even before the boxes were unpacked!

If we needed any more convincing that God was with us, this came in the form of two young guys who lived in the immediate vicinity. Both had been volunteers with the initial group that ran The FUSE; one had helped install all the IT systems and proved absolutely invaluable in helping us get everything working. The other was the son of the parish vicar and was a trained youth worker. Both felt called to resign their jobs and offer themselves as full-time interns until we were able to employ them properly. We made contact with local housing associations and other groups who helped us financially by sponsoring new community activities and hiring space for their own training sessions. One group helped us recruit a receptionist and even paid her full-time salary for a year.

One big lesson for us was that even though God was absolutely in charge of this miracle, the enemy was not going to leave us alone. The opposition we faced came as a huge surprise to us. There were factions in the community that had always opposed the way that The FUSE had been run from its very inception. Unbelievably, some had seen the failure of the initial charity as a victory and had felt that they would now be offered the building. Although this was a small minority, who had no valid credentials, they mounted a campaign to try to derail the whole thing. We tried to talk to them in the hope that we could work together for the benefit of the community but they seemed interested only in making life difficult for us. There were many negative comments made on social media, especially focusing on our Christian values. In some ways, I was happy to accept that we would always attract opposition because of our God-centred vision, but I've always tried hard to follow Jesus' example and find favour with both God and people as far as possible (Luke 2.52). At the time of writing, four years after moving in, we've won over most of our opponents, largely by demonstrating that we're prepared to work flat out to keep the place going as a community asset, including providing many activities at no cost for local residents and subsidising many local groups who use the centre.

Biblical examples

Divine favour features throughout the Bible: Joseph gained unprecedented prominence in Egypt due to his God-given gifts of dream interpretation, Pharoah made him ruler of the whole country and granted him astonishing privileges (Genesis 41.38–44); the Israelites leaving Egypt were given jewels, gold and clothing as a demonstration of God's favour (Exodus 12.36); Daniel and his friends were honoured by the king in the midst of their adversaries (Daniel 2.48–49); Esther was given prominence and preferential treatment, and her petitions were granted by ungodly, secular authorities. And, although divine favour is entirely bestowed by God's own sovereign choice, there do seem to be some common principles that precede it, especially a strong determination to honour God and trust him to move mountains.

My favourite example is that of Nehemiah who, like Daniel, was a captive in Babylon during the exile and served in the royal court. The city of Jerusalem had been completely destroyed and the remnant of Jews who were not taken away into captivity were suffering greatly at the hands of their local enemies who were able to plunder the city because of its broken walls. Years ago, God gave a picture to a group of us as we prayed for Manchester, in which we 'saw' our city in a similar state. The interpretation was that the spiritual fabric of our city had been eroded and the devil was attacking the inhabitants without resistance. From this we began to pray that the Church would rebuild the spiritual defences through united prayer – the whole story is told in our first book, *City-Changing Prayer*.

Nehemiah was so moved by the personal reports he received from contacts who visited Jerusalem that he wept and mourned for days. As he prayed and fasted, he developed a strong vision for the rebuilding of the city. God answered by causing the king to take a personal interest and he asked Nehemiah to let him know exactly what was needed to tackle the problems. I would love to be able to ask Nehemiah about the mountain-moving prayer he so briefly refers to in Nehemiah 2.4 (AMPC): 'The king said to me, "What is it you want?" Then I prayed to the God of heaven.' It looks like an arrow prayer to me. He only appears to have a split second to pray before going on, 'If it pleases the king and if your servant has found favour in his sight, let him send me to the city in Judah where my ancestors are buried so that I can rebuild it.' The king immediately agrees without any objection at all. So Nehemiah wades in to take advantage of the divinely opened door; he asks for royal protection on the journey and all the necessary materials to repair the gates and walls: 'And because the gracious hand of my God was on me, the king granted my requests.' Provision does indeed follow vision!

Once we'd properly moved into The FUSE we had a day of prayer to dedicate the building to the Lord. A ROC-supporting vicar from Blackpool, Steve Haskett, came along to pray with us. He told us that he felt God had a message for us. He put a bunch of keys into Frank's hands and said, 'You will receive many other buildings like this around the UK.' Then he prayed over our team. It seemed quite a crazy prayer as far as we were concerned. We'd only just got the keys to The FUSE! We hadn't yet even worked out how we would pay for the utilities or staff. It looked as though we would need at least two more staff, a caretaker and receptionist. Now we were hearing about more miracle provision. We're open to this happening if God ordains it; we've learnt now to trust him when we feel out of our depth, so bring it on Lord! We have plenty of partners around the country with the vision and faith to collaborate with us on more miraculous mountain-moving projects.

Case studies

As Steve said, God would open other doors to buildings. We heard a bit about Marike from Dawlish earlier in this book. Here is a story about Mark, her dad, that demonstrates divine favour and potential partnerships.

Dawlish – he said 'Build'

In 2011 Mark was feeling burned out. Seeking the Lord one day at Rame Head in south-east Cornwall, he felt that the Holy Spirit spoke one powerful, empowering word: 'Build'. Ian Williams, an Assemblies of God pastor and friend, shared the same word with him and put him in touch with ROC.

But God was also talking to others. John and Tracey German, friends of Mark and his wife Jo, had a vision about a new church community centre in a field on the outskirts of Dawlish. They said nothing to anyone. In the meantime, Mark had become chaplain to the new mayor. Over coffee one day, the mayor showed him the plans for a new housing development on the edge of town. The development had a Section 106 provision – a multipurpose community facility. The land was available for £1! Later that day Mark shared this with John and Tracey. Suddenly the prophetic words they had both received began to make sense. They had been wondering if they ever would.

With planning permission now in place and funds available from their building sale, grants and legacies, the Dawlish centre is close to becoming a reality as we write this book. It was not without its struggles. But God had some reassurance for them along the way.

During a 60-mile charity walk, Mark felt the Lord was impressing on him the word 'Allenby'. Alex, a pastor friend, contacted him around that time and urged him to listen to the Lord very carefully on the walk. Mark did some research and found that during the Great War, in 1917, General Edmund Allenby was charged with taking Jerusalem from the Turks. Reading his story quickly led Mark to Isaiah 31.5, the verse that the Lord had given to the general outside the walls of Jerusalem:

> Like birds hovering overhead,
> the LORD Almighty will shield Jerusalem;
> he will shield it and deliver it,
> he will 'pass over' it and will rescue it.

The birds mentioned in that verse reminded Jo of the names of the roads at the Warren Grove site for our building – all named after birds (Swift, Kestrel, Black Swan etc.). Deep in the night, a few weeks later, as Mark tossed and turned in his sleeplessness, he had a revelation – the phrase 'I've got this covered', with its echoes of Isaiah 31.5, was impressed on him. With the £1 land deal looking shaky at the time, this word of comfort helped Mark and the congregation to press on. God heaped on the nudges towards faith and perseverance. A church member's painting, which spoke of both the town and the sense of the winding path it depicted, was like their journey as a church, and it won a prize, the Allenby Award.

Mark felt moved to write a prayer of faith about the '£1 land' in the prayer request book at Salisbury cathedral during a visit. A few minutes later a tour guide asked him if he needed help or information. Her name was Allenby. She was a distant relative of the General and shared more information about him than Mark had previously known. Mark comments: 'At times like this, I have to ask, whom are we dealing with who has this level of kindness, this attention to detail, and this sense of comic timing?'

Richard Gamble and the wall of answered prayer

I'll let Richard tell his story of vision and provision:

> We are building a national landmark about answered prayer, and
> we need land next to a motorway, which is very expensive, and we

have limited resources. During a visit to Bethel church in Redding, California, we received a prophetic word that 'God has some heavenly land prepared for you'.

Another member of his team felt a word impressed on her one day while brushing her teeth. She researched the word and found a dental practice, looked above it and saw a motorway and a piece of land.

> She was unaware that two weeks previously that landowner had emailed me and asked to meet. I shared the vision with him and he informed me about a trust fund set up 14 and a half years ago (6 months before I received the vision for the project). This fund was created to support a project that wanted to build a national landmark about Jesus – this was an incredible connection through a word of knowledge. Fast forward a few months and he has given us a ten-acre piece of land right next to a motorway.

There were more miracles to come as they sought the funds to build. Richard told an old friend, as they met for the first time in 28 years, about the wall.

> A few days later, he texted to inform me that he could not stop thinking about the project and thought it was an amazing idea – this is miraculous in itself as he is not a Christian. He told some Christian friends about the project who are in very high positions in London, which led to a number of meetings with wealthy Christians who are gradually coming on board with the vision and helping with the financing. I asked my friend why he had contacted me randomly after 28 years and he said that my name had popped into his head while he was walking across London Bridge.

From the vision flows provision. But then God sends us the last, the least and the lost.

9

Wedding bells

It all started a few weeks ago when I found a diamond ring in one of the many car parks at the Trafford Centre. To give you an idea of size and scale, the car park has 11,500 car park spaces!

This is not my story but was told to me by my friend Helen Wrigley. Let me share the rest of it and what I believe it's teaching us.

It was such a lovely ring, but I didn't feel I should just hand it in. So I put a message out on social media. It was some time before I heard anything.

A lovely lady contacted me who had spent many hours looking for the ring. In fact she had lost two rings, her engagement and wedding rings, after taking the rings off while moisturizing her hands in the car. They had jumped off her lap when she got out of the car.

A few weeks later she and her newly-wed husband decided to go to church, something they didn't normally do. They went to Ivy Church in Manchester and heard a sermon on miracles. The congregation were then invited to stick Post-it notes on a cross at the front, with specific prayer-request miracles. The lady, of course, asked God to find her rings.

After the service, she noticed the post I put out about the ring as we had some friends in common and she contacted me. Amazingly, it was her engagement ring! She then returned to the car park and, you won't believe this, her wedding ring was still there two weeks later!

Within a few hours of asking God, she found both her rings! Helen sent me this message recently:

The thing I have since learnt is that when the couple returned to look for the ring in the car park (after we had messaged her), the ring was not in the place they had parked the car . . . it had somehow found its way onto the road outside the car park, and after looking for it without success they decided to just check the road outside the car park! Amazing. The other thing is, this couple had their wedding reception at The Message Trust Enterprise Centre. I understand that her parents are Christians (and have no doubt been praying for her).

Finding the lost

God is in the business of finding the lost! Time in prayer is a massive key in this process. We get to partner with God in an incredible way. Sometimes our part in the partnership is to pray and listen, and sometimes we also have to go to work to 'find the lost'. This is a key insight for us at ROC as we always seek both to pray and to act. Jesus tells three stories about the lost that help us.

> Now the tax collectors and sinners were all gathering around to hear Jesus. But the Pharisees and the teachers of the law muttered, 'This man welcomes sinners and eats with them.'
>
> Then Jesus told them this parable: 'Suppose one of you has a hundred sheep and loses one of them. Doesn't he leave the ninety-nine in the open country and go after the lost sheep until he finds it? And when he finds it, he joyfully puts it on his shoulders and goes home. Then he calls his friends and neighbours together and says, "Rejoice with me; I have found my lost sheep." I tell you that in the same way there will be more rejoicing in heaven over one sinner who repents than over ninety-nine righteous people who do not need to repent.
>
> 'Or suppose a woman has ten silver coins and loses one. Doesn't she light a lamp, sweep the house and search carefully until she finds it? And when she finds it, she calls her friends and neighbours together and says, "Rejoice with me; I have found my lost coin." In the same way, I tell you, there is rejoicing in the presence of the angels of God over one sinner who repents.'   (Luke 15.1–10)

Both stories speak to us of the desire to find the lost item or animal. For the woman who lost the coin, it was an urgent matter. This was part of her 'insurance fund' for emergencies and times of bad harvests. For the shepherd seeking the sheep there was probably more than his own needs to think of. His own sheep were in the herd, but he was probably looking after sheep that belonged to others as well.

There is a sense of urgency, but there is also a note of rejoicing in both stories. We may sow in tears, but we reap in joy.

The notes of both urgency and rejoicing reach a crescendo in the story of the lost son, as we're reminded of the heart attitude that underlies our passion for the lost – a love that is unmerited but relentlessly merciful.

Everlasting love

Jesus continued: 'There was a man who had two sons. The younger one said to his father, "Father, give me my share of the estate." So he divided his property between them.

'Not long after that, the younger son got together all he had, set off for a distant country and there squandered his wealth in wild living. After he had spent everything, there was a severe famine in that whole country, and he began to be in need. So he went and hired himself out to a citizen of that country, who sent him to his fields to feed pigs. He longed to fill his stomach with the pods that the pigs were eating, but no one gave him anything.

'When he came to his senses, he said, "How many of my father's hired servants have food to spare, and here I am starving to death! I will set out and go back to my father and say to him: Father, I have sinned against heaven and against you. I am no longer worthy to be called your son; make me like one of your hired servants." So he got up and went to his father.

'But while he was still a long way off, his father saw him and was filled with compassion for him; he ran to his son, threw his arms around him and kissed him.

'The son said to him, "Father, I have sinned against heaven and against you. I am no longer worthy to be called your son."

'But the father said to his servants, "Quick! Bring the best robe and put it on him. Put a ring on his finger and sandals on his feet. Bring the fattened calf and kill it. Let's have a feast and celebrate. For this son of mine was dead and is alive again; he was lost and is found." So they began to celebrate.'   (Luke 15.11–24)

Whole books have been written about this one parable alone. There's much that we could say about the other brother as well. But let us focus on just one character, the father.

- Despite being 'wished dead' by the inheritance request, he loved the one he had lost.
- Despite his age, he set aside the dignity expected of him, hitched up his robes and ran to his returning son.
- Despite the fact that he could have desired vengeance, he protected his son with the kiss of welcome.
- Despite all the son had done, he gave him a lavish reception, bringing him back into the family in a celebratory way.

This lavish, selfless love of God for lost people is exactly what motivates the work of ROC and, despite all that would deter, anger or thwart us, his joyful, unconditional love is the fuel that powers the mountain-moving prayer we rely on to see transformation come. This is how we experience both divine favour and community favour. When we embody his love people catch a glimpse of Jesus and his relentless love. I heard a preacher once say, 'If you don't love your community, don't do any outreach; instead get on your knees and ask God to share his love for the community with you.'

Esther – lived-out love

We've already seen that Nehemiah experienced divine favour. Nehemiah was prepared to answer the king's question. He spent time seeking God's face in prayer and had a ready answer. Esther also found favour with the King and was able to speak out for her community.

> On the third day Esther put on her royal robes and stood in the inner court of the palace, in front of the king's hall. The king was sitting on his royal throne in the hall, facing the entrance. When he saw Queen Esther standing in the court, he was pleased with her and held out to her the gold sceptre that was in his hand. So Esther approached and touched the tip of the sceptre.
>
> Then the king asked, 'What is it, Queen Esther? What is your request? Even up to half the kingdom, it will be given you.'
>
> 'If it pleases the king,' replied Esther, 'let the king, together with Haman, come today to a banquet I have prepared for him.'
>
> 'Bring Haman at once,' the king said, 'so that we may do what Esther asks.'

> So the king and Haman went to the banquet Esther had prepared. As they were drinking wine, the king again asked Esther, 'Now what is your petition? It will be given you. And what is your request? Even up to half the kingdom, it will be granted.'
>
> Esther replied, 'My petition and my request is this: If the king regards me with favour and if it pleases the king to grant my petition and fulfil my request, let the king and Haman come tomorrow to the banquet I will prepare for them. Then I will answer the king's question.' (Esther 5.1–8)

The book of Esther is a dramatic account that can give us insight into God's special and purposeful plan for our lives. The story gives us six powerful lessons about courage, divine timing and God's supreme love. As Scripture reveals, Esther is a Jewish woman living in Persia and reared by her cousin Mordecai. She was taken to the king of the Persian Empire to become a part of his harem but, because there was something special about Esther, he made her queen. Mordecai, however, didn't tell the king about a major detail, Esther's Jewish heritage. She puts her life at risk to plead for her people – you could not enter the presence of the king without being invited.

Writer and speaker Lisa Brown Ross captures these six lessons in a short but inspirational list.

Lesson 1: God has a plan for our lives. Mordecai nailed it when he said: 'For if you remain silent at this time, relief and deliverance for the Jews will arise from another place, but you and your father's family will perish. And who knows but that you have come to your royal position for such a time as this?' (Esther 4.14). God loved the Jewish people. And, he didn't create Esther's beauty and finesse for her and her alone. Esther was placed in a royal position to assist in the delivery of God's divine plan.

Lesson 2: We're given divine moments to alter circumstances. As believers, there are no such things as accidents or coincidences. God's timing is providential. Esther's divine moment of providence came by accepting her responsibility to go to the king. However, Mordecai was clear when he said to Esther that she could be the one who saved the people, or not. God will use you only if you're ready – or he will find someone else.

Lesson 3: We must stand with courage. 'I will go to the king, even though it is against the law. And if I perish, I perish' (Esther 4.16). Esther was willing to die to save her people. Sometimes we must stand in courage, even when it is not popular to do so, and risk it all.

Lesson 4: Fasting and prayer brings clarity and hope for deliverance. God is not mentioned in the book of Esther even once. But Esther was clear that in this particular situation, a heavenly response was needed for an earthly situation. Esther needed direction. When we need God's grace, fasting and prayer opens the portals for spiritual growth, removes distractions and places us on a path to humility.

Lesson 5: God demands obedience. Esther's obedience saved God's people from genocide. The reality is that Esther didn't know what would happen when she approached the king. She acted in obedience, and by doing so she saved a nation and received the best. We don't get a pass on this one.

Lesson 6: God uses everything and everybody for his divine purpose. No part of our lives is untouched. God is in control of every aspect, whether we want him to be or not, and there is nothing that is not subject to him (Hebrews 2.8). And, the best thing we can do for our lives is to search for and surrender to his will.

(Ross, '6 Powerful Lessons from the Book of Esther')

Esther said, 'I and my attendants will fast as you do. When this is done, I will go to the king, even though it is against the law. And if I perish, I perish' (Esther 4.16).

There are moments in history when a door for massive change opens. Great revolutions, either good or evil, spring up in the vacuum created by these openings. In such divine moments, key men, women and entire generations risk everything to become the hinge of history – the 'pivot point' that determines which way the door will swing.

The Esther hour

Esther is a prototype of history's hinge – a courageous woman who humbly and artfully spoke truth to power. Facing witchcraft and dark conspiracies at the highest levels of Persia's power base, Queen

Esther found herself providentially positioned (right place, right time) to risk everything for the love of her people and their future. Armed with little more than her dignity and the secret arsenal of corporate prayer and fasting, her courageous actions spared an entire nation from annihilation. Like Daniel and Joseph, she found herself at the heart of the nation's affairs and with an opportunity to speak wisdom and mercy to the king.

Armed with our dignity, our passion for prayer and the empowerment of the Holy Spirit, will we be an Esther- or Daniel-type figure for our communities?

Royal favour

The year 2018 was one of royal connections for ROC. In January, Her Royal Highness the Princess Royal came to visit The FUSE to celebrate five years of our restorative justice project. In May 2018 I was invited to attend the wedding of Prince Harry and Meghan Markle at Windsor Castle. And in June we heard that we'd been awarded the Queen's Award for voluntary service, which involved an invitation to Buckingham Palace for a garden party.

The royal connections didn't come as a huge surprise. In 2017 we received a number of prophetic words that such things would happen. No details, just a number of different people on different occasions sharing that they believed God was going to show us favour in royal circles.

What was quite a surprise, though, was my daughter Sarah being named as a Meghan Markle look-a-like! She was in Ikea when she was first approached: 'Do you know that you look like Meghan?' She didn't know who Meghan was! Frank and I were more clued up as we were watching the TV series *Suits*, in which she plays one of the lead characters. We often used to comment on the likeness, but didn't think any more about it until the news of her engagement broke and the media began to contact Sarah, offering photo opportunities. Demand was high so she registered with an agent.

As the big day dawned, the assignments flooded in and she was asked to appear on the TV show *This Morning* with Eamonn Holmes. Then the show found out that I had been invited to the wedding because of my work with ROC. They thought it was quite amusing that I was going to the wedding and my daughter looked like the bride! So we appeared on the show. We even met the royal florist and were both presented with a bridal bouquet. Sarah was also on *Loose Women*, and ROC got a mention and a big round of applause.

It was a privilege to be among the guests who were invited inside the castle grounds to see the wedding processions, the amazing outfits and meet some lovely people. We sat with the Queen's dresser and talked with her about the Queen's wardrobe. The service had so many special moments, including the huge cheer from around the castle grounds when Meghan said 'I do'! It was also interesting to discuss Michael Curry's message with guests near me. Most were not really used to such lively, engaging preaching but his message about the power of love really drew them in. The message was reinforced when a London-based choir, the Kingdom Choir, sang Ben E. King's 'Stand by me', a song inspired by the classic hymn, 'Lord, stand by me'.

There's something strong, wise and beautiful about the love God has for us and desires us to share with others.

> Place me like a seal over your heart,
>   like a seal on your arm;
> for love is as strong as death,
>   its jealousy unyielding as the grave.
> It burns like blazing fire,
>   like a mighty flame.
> Many waters cannot quench love;
>   rivers cannot sweep it away.
> If one were to give
>   all the wealth of one's house for love,
>   it would be utterly scorned.
>   (Song of Songs 8.6–7)

First Corinthians 13 reminds us that 'love never fails'. This love has character, not just feelings.

> If I speak in the tongues of men or of angels, but do not have love, I am only a resounding gong or a clanging cymbal. If I have the gift of prophecy and can fathom all mysteries and all knowledge, and if I have a faith that can move mountains, but do not have love, I am

nothing. If I give all I possess to the poor and give over my body to hardship that I may boast, but do not have love, I gain nothing.

Love is patient, love is kind. It does not envy, it does not boast, it is not proud, it does not dishonor others, it is not self-seeking, it is not easily angered, it keeps no record of wrongs. Love does not delight in evil but rejoices with the truth. It always protects, always trusts, always hopes, always perseveres.

Love never fails.   (1 Corinthians 13.1–8)

Mountain-moving faith must be seasoned with love

A royal visit, a trip to Buckingham Palace and an invitation to the royal wedding in the space of a few months certainly caused a stir in our office! But we have access to a heavenly King who grants us a relationship with him and access to the presence of God 24/7. His love is eternal in the way no human earthly love can ever be. Why do we believe this?

- Abba Father – Jesus' use of the word Abba in the Lord's Prayer reframes our relationship with God as a warm, familial relationship. We can know we are loved.
- Adopted into family – this familial love is reinforced by Paul who reminds us that 'the Spirit you received brought about your adoption to sonship. And by him we cry, "*Abba*, Father"' (Romans 8.15).
- Commissioned for service – Peter tells us, 'You are a chosen people, a royal priesthood, a holy nation. God's special possession' (1 Peter 2.9). Being adopted gives you responsibilities and rights. Being part of a priesthood also carries rights and responsibilities.
- Secure in his presence – God welcomes us into his presence: 'Let us then approach God's throne of grace with confidence' (Hebrews 4.16).
- Secure in his promise – God is ready and willing to respond to us and promises us that we will 'receive mercy and find grace to help us in our time of need' (Hebrews 4.16).

Love has character. Love has purpose. Love is full of wisdom. Love is emotional and warm and sensitive to the brokenness inside us and others. It is a rich and wonderful thing. The Love Command is a striking melody in the song of Jesus: 'A new command I give you: love one another. As I have loved you, so you must love one another. By this everyone will know that you are my disciples, if you love one another' (John 13.34–35).

Having prayed, you can now take action, because what you have prayed will have moved you to action. Your thinking will have been renewed, your heart will have been stirred, your imagination will have started to dream God's dreams for the place where you live. So now what will you do?

Here are six Esther- or Daniel-type ideas to spark your imagination and spur you to action.

1 Write a letter to your MP – not a complaint, but an affirmation of something he or she has done for your area.
2 Sign a petition about an issue in your locality.
3 Start a campaign to save something people value, or bring something new to your area.
4 Visit someone in prison.
5 Open your home to an asylum seeker. (Jesus' family sought asylum in Egypt.)
6 Volunteer for a community project – anything that encourages connection, conversation and community.

You can find 101 ideas like this in our community manual. Visit www.roc.uk.com/mmp.

When you pray and act, God's name starts to become famous for goodness where you live.

Establishing divine strongholds

We're aware of the spiritual darkness that can surround us. But we can live in the light of the biblical promise that 'the one who is in us is greater than the one who is in the world' (1 John 4.4). As Alan Scott reminds us, let us think about the divine strongholds that God establishes through his people, for the sake of the lost and broken. Let us look to the things he has done in the past and believe that his works of mercy, compassion and love will again call our communities away from destruction and towards wisdom and restoration.

Imagine that you're walking around the town or district where you live. You pass the job centre, an idea that started with William Booth and the Salvation Army. A bit further down the road is the probation office, a restorative justice idea that was founded by Christians. You wander into the park that was originally funded by an Anglican philanthropist and past the now in-demand nineteenth-century workers' accommodation she also funded.

You drop into the hospital to see a friend and notice the plaque that indicates that this was originally the All Saints Hospital. Off in the distance you can see the church that sponsored it and the still-flourishing school beside it.

But you need some cash, so you pop into Barclays or Lloyds. These were founded by Quakers who wanted to finance the dreams of the ordinary worker or small business man or woman. It being Saturday you meet your son and daughter outside the ground of your local team, which grew out of the boys' club in the local mission hall.

The fingerprints of generations who valued community cohesion and engagement are all around us. God desires to raise up new arenas for the Holy Spirit in the town where you live, for the sake of his name and because of his great love. God raises up everyday people to do the simple acts of love that often start the heart change for those who do not know him yet. God raises up Esther- and Daniel-type people who will use their influence to help nurture, protect and restore communities.

We're not called to do it alone. We need to find the place of commanded blessing as we bring the love of God to our communities. What has God shown us about unity, prayer and blessing?

10

Prayer partnerships

It's always been a massive encouragement to me that ROC was born out of a united prayer gathering. Our regional launch took place at the Reebok stadium in Bolton in 2004. Our national launch came only two years later at the NEC in Birmingham in 2006. It was part of the Trumpet Call Prayer event hosted by the World Prayer Centre (WPC). I'm so grateful to Ian and Pauline Cole for inviting us to launch ROC in the middle of their prayer day.

My good friend Nick, the dreaming vicar, had a dream a few days before about a large number of Christians praying for the police. He saw thousands with outstretched arms praying over what appeared to be an officer directing traffic on a busy road. I didn't fully understand it but knew it related to the launch at the Trumpet Call.

During the launch I was interviewing some police officers, including Sir Matt Baggott who was Chief Constable of Leicester back then. Matt is a Christian and has had a huge influence on the shape of policing across the nation. When we had finished talking, I had the sudden impulse to invite all officers and civilians in the police force to come forward. Forty people filed to the front of the arena. We prayed for their safety and protection. We asked for wisdom for them in their role in community well-being and crime reduction. When I opened my eyes I saw 7,000 hands outstretched towards them. Nick's dream suddenly made sense.

We have a great relationship with the Christian Police Association (CPA). We've run community events in partnership with the CPA recently in Thanet, Nuneaton, Canterbury and Tavistock, and have plans for Norwich and Northampton. It's a marriage made in heaven as we share so much in common in our desire to behave with integrity and compassion in our communities. (As we wrote this I discovered that Dave, my co-author, is the son of a former General Secretary of CPA, George Roberts. George had worked with others to help broaden the vision of CPA from fellowship and witness to engagement with the wider issues within the police and the community that faced many officers every day – their work is bearing fruit!)

We returned to the Trumpet Call ten years later in 2016. This time ROC was getting ready to go international and we were just about to launch in Australia. The whole gathering prayed over us and commissioned us for a new task. This time the World Prayer Centre had invited a number of organizations to stand together in unity, including Hope Together, Cinnamon Network, Gather UK, Open Doors and ROC. It was a wonderful demonstration of unity as each organization prayed for the others.

We remind ourselves often that, in the words of A. T. Pierson, 'There has never been a spiritual awakening in any country or locality that did not begin in united prayer.' Prayer can be a solitary activity, but praying with others moves more mountains!

What is the prayer of agreement, and how do we discover who are our partners? How can we pray together with purpose and clarity? What fruits does partnership produce? Here are some of our experiences.

We stand together in Cheshire

In early 2017, I had an appointment with the Chief Constable of Cheshire. We discussed the idea of bringing faith groups together to talk about partnerships that would lead to community action. He bought us together with the Police and Crime Commissioner of Cheshire, David Keane.

We then agreed to help organize a Cheshire-wide conference for all eight districts of the county under the banner of 'We stand together in Cheshire'. A reflective process where we shared our key beliefs was suggested as a way of promoting tolerance and good relations. Reminding ourselves how we were different didn't sound to me like a partnership promoting strategy, so I suggested that we focus on community needs and the things we wanted to achieve together. Thankfully that was agreed.

In November 2017, 200 people gathered in a local hotel. The

police were happy – a previous attempt to gather the faith communities had only attracted 35 attendees. We featured case studies from across Cheshire, which highlighted the high engagement of many church and faith groups with their local community. People from each district then talked together and established goals for the following year. Six months later we had tracked over 20 new pieces of community work that came directly from the conference. These include the launch of a new street pastors group in Crewe, a new ROC Centre community hub in Wilmslow, and a mentoring scheme for young people. Chester has hosted a civic leaders' prayer breakfast. The ROC team in Lymm have been successful in taking over the local library as a community centre and social enterprise. A gathering focused on enabling partnerships and fostering unity enabled all these ideas to move forward.

We need to talk about talking

ROC was launched in Northern Ireland in 2012. We've already shared in this book about some of their projects. This work has led us into an exciting partnership with the Department of Justice and the Police Service of Northern Ireland. We are currently developing strategic partnerships with churches, both Catholic and Protestant, across the region with a view to hold eight key community engagement events over the next three years.

Prayer has played a vital role in the process. The leader of ROC in Northern Ireland, Keeva Watson, has organized weekly prayer gatherings at the Vine Centre on Crumlin Road. A WhatsApp group gets regular prayer alerts and prayers are being answered on a daily basis. Approaching change via conversations, rather than prepared solutions is vital in a community where the emotional, social and physical wounds run deep.

The Holts conversation – from committee tables to café tables

Following the ROC Conversation in Holts, Oldham, in September 2017, we discovered that there was a lack of community spaces in the area.

We joined a 'place based' initiative, the Holts and Lees Community team, which has brought together 15 different agencies to address the social issues on the estate. The community space was in a converted shop. Initially we were successful in raising some funds to employ two part-time staff to help coordinate activities in the area. Team workers Kaylee and Donna rolled up their sleeves to create a community café.

But the café is quite small and regularly has over 50 visitors – we needed more space. The answer lay with our successful 20-year partnership with Greater Manchester Police. Superintendent Danny Inglis put an application into the proceeds of crime fund and we were awarded £100,000 to build an extension to the café! The bell was ringing in our office on the day we received that news. The whole process has been aided by another great partnership with First Choice homes, one of the local social housing providers who, like many others around the country, have a strong desire to make communities safer, kinder and stronger. In many cases, this is part of the mission statement of the organization and often there is money available to support action projects such as these.

A team from Holts recently went to visit our well-established café and community centre in Edgeley, the Olive ROC Centre, and were able to gain inspiration from them. As someone once said, 'Why reinvent the wheel?' And prayer has been a key factor, with Donna organizing regular prayer meetings with all the local Oldham churches. The Holts estate does not have its own church yet but at the time of writing plans are being discussed. Community engagement is often the place, however, where a church builds firm foundations in a community.

A tale of five treasurers

We needed to raise £1.5 million for a city-wide mission to Manchester. During a time of prayer I felt prompted to go to the highest point of the city to pray. Of course, we have no mountains in Manchester! The highest point, in those days, was the CIS tower, home to the Co-operative, 24 storeys high, and the workplace for 2,000 employees. My friend Peter told me that they had a Christian Union meeting every Friday on the top floor!

So my prayer partner Wendy and I arrived one Friday to meet on the top floor with five Christian men who worked there. We prayed very specifically for the release of finances for the mission. At the end of the prayer time the five guys were all pretty quiet. I was worried in case it was our prayer style that had offended them. Peter eventually offered the reason. He said, 'We were shocked that you came here especially to pray for finances. You see, each one of us goes to a different church but we all have the same role. We are all church treasurers!' And yes, a few weeks later all the funds needed for the mission were raised. Hundreds of people had been praying for the same thing, including five church treasurers – a perfect example of the prayer of agreement.

Compassion provokes partnerships; prayer provokes provision

We moved to our £5 million miracle headquarters on 29 July 2014. The miraculous provision of this state-of-the-art community and conference centre was one of the clearest answers to prayer I have ever experienced. We have a long-term, rent-free lease but we face the challenge of raising £100,000 per year to keep the place running. I remember feeling very nervous when I signed the contract. How would we pay the utility bills? How would we pay for extra staff? What about repairs and maintenance costs?

I can honestly say that we have prayed every step of the way since we first got the keys. God has been faithful and has provided in so many ways, albeit sometimes at the last minute. We are truly living by faith. We now have around 25 different community projects running in the building and thousands have visited over the past year. God provided a caretaker and a receptionist quite miraculously as a result of our relationship with local partner agencies. We currently subsidise all local community groups by providing our premises free of charge. Last year's (2017's) value of these subsidies was £88,470. It's fantastic to be able to support the community in this way.

The fruit of partnership is everywhere to be seen. But sometimes a call to unity and partnership can be strong on sentiment but low on the basic building blocks of fruitful partnership. What are those building blocks?

1 Giving your neighbourhood a new (reputational) name. Jerusalem had a personality and a reputation for hard-heartedness and violence against the people of God. Jesus wept over the city: 'Jerusalem, Jerusalem, you who kill the prophets and stone those sent to you, how often I have longed to gather your children together, as a hen gathers her chicks under her wings, and you were not willing' (Matthew 23.37).

This reputational naming is important for good and bad reasons. The Lancashire town of Accrington, not far from here in the North-West, is known as 'Tacky Accy'. These nicknames stick long after situations have changed. Jesus and his disciples came from Galilee, not an area held in high regard by the Jerusalem elite. Nathaniel wondered out loud: 'Can any good thing come from Nazareth?' But Jesus created his own reputation for goodness, because he was present to and near the ordinary people. They trusted him for his wisdom, because of his healings and because of his unconditional love.

Community change begins with a church that is trusted, wise and embraces its community. This in turn leads eventually to a new reputation for that place. What new reputation is our work in unity and partnership seeking? What new story will we start to tell so that a fresh vision can be released for where we live?

2 Jesus and the prayer of agreement. I believe our collective prayers add weight to our requests in heaven. We show our agreement in our ordinary prayer habits and in our use of the word Amen. Amen means I agree, so be it. Jesus tells us that agreement is powerful:

> 'Again, truly I tell you that if two of you on earth agree about any-thing they ask for, it will be done for them by my Father in heaven. For where two or three gather in my name, there am I with them.'
>
> (Matthew 18.19–20)

Bible teacher and pastor John Hamel, commenting on this passage, notes:

> The word that Jesus used for 'agree' in the above verse literally means 'to stipulate (demand) by contract, to arrange definitively

by covenant'. Therefore, when Jesus said 'If two of you shall agree', He was actually saying, 'If two of you will stipulate (place a demand upon) our arranged contract or covenant . . .'

The word that Jesus used for 'thing' in the above verse actually means 'a deed'. A deed is a legal contract that transfers possessions from one party to another party. Here the deed that Jesus refers to is the Bible, our Covenant or Contract with Almighty God.

Now, reading the verse in context according to our two word definitions, we see more clearly that Jesus was actually saying, 'If two or three of you shall place a demand on anything that is written in the Covenant Contract Deed, My Father will personally see to it that it is transferred from His possession to yours.'

(Hamel, 'How and When to Pray the Prayer of Agreement')

3 Partnership is best founded on relational connection. Prayer and transformation are like two boats in the water. Working together in a common task, they then form a perfect partnership. Jesus taught the disciples to pray with unity always in mind:

> 'This, then, is how you should pray:
> "Our Father in heaven,
> hallowed be your name."'
>
> (Matthew 6.9)

'Ask the Lord of the harvest therefore to send out workers into his harvest field.'   (Matthew 9.38)

In some editions of the Bible, Luke 5.1–11 is subtitled 'The miraculous catch of fish', but it could equally be referred to as 'The miraculous partnerships'.

> When they had [let down the nets], they caught such a large number of fish that their nets began to break. So they signalled their partners in the other boat to come and help them, and they came and filled both boats so full that they began to sink.   (Luke 5.6–7)

This raises a significant question for us today: who are our partners in the other boat?

> When we pray, we participate in the most dramatic partnership of creation and recreation. The partnership with God that involves gazing on his creation – on the events of the world he has made –

and seeking that they be conformed to his likeness and image. We are changed, and the world is changed, as God allows us, through prayer, to share in his making of the world. We are his partners in making the world, in prayer.

Jean Vanier, who founded the L'Arche communities, said: 'To pray is essentially to come to Jesus and to drink.'

(Welby, 'Prayer Is a Partnership with God')

Partnerships are not built on a mere process of meeting and agreeing an agenda, but on relationships. The healthiest partnerships often grow from strong relationship foundations.

These strong relationships often spring from eating together, hearing stories about life and faith and community, laughing together, talking about our families or the football. We share something of who we are, and partnerships are established. We learn from each other.

The great unity psalm captures something of how being engaged with people is a part of the partnership unity matrix.

Behold, how good and how pleasant it is for brethren to *dwell together* in unity!

It is like the precious ointment upon the head, that ran down upon the beard, even Aaron's beard: that went down to the skirts of his garments;

As the dew of Hermon, and as the dew that descended upon the mountains of Zion: for there the Lord commanded the blessing, even life for evermore. (Psalm 133, KJV)

Dwell is one of those words that has layers of meaning. It can mean where you live. But it has a flavour of slowing down and meditating together around a common interest.

Prayer, then, is about sharing every part of yourself and your life with God. Praying together brings that divine partnership into our human partnerships and helps us create community, not merely from a plan but because we are a community in every fibre of our being and desire to draw others into community.

We've compiled many practical questions that will help you reflect on unity, partnership and your city. These will be in the ROC prayer course materials that are a companion to this book (see the back pages of this book for more information). But here are some key principles derived from the teaching of Jesus that have helped us as we pray together.

> 'Again, truly I tell you that if two of you on earth agree about any-thing they ask for, it will be done for them by my Father in heaven. For where two or three gather in my name, there am I with them.'
>
> (Matthew 18.19–20)

- Be clear about what you want. You can't ask for one thing, but really want another. This will create doubt.
- Be specific. If you want more money, for example, you need to know how much money you want and why you want it.
- Clearly state your request to those praying with you to ensure that they are praying in harmony with what you want.
- Choose the person or persons carefully whom you'll be praying with. Make sure they understand this prayer and the principles of the 'prayer of faith'.
- Choose people who have your best interest at heart. You can't pray with someone just because they're a Christian and you need someone to pray with you. You would do better to pray alone. You need prayer partners who are totally in agreement with you and want you to be blessed.
- Be honest about your situation. God knows the truth when we go before him.
- Continue to thank God that he has answered your prayer once you've prayed.

Dreaming for your city

We see the fruit of partnership, we understand the heart of God about unity, community and the power of agreement. Now we start to think about the actual realities of our city, town or neighbourhood.

There are a number of mission thinkers who will take us gently out of our comfort zone and help us think about God's heart for our cities and towns.

John Dawson, influential in the early days of 24-7 Prayer and an elder statesman in Youth With A Mission, is eloquent in this respect. He opens up for us a new way to look at our city. He states the obvious first, then draws some surprising inferences. The obvious is this: 'I believe God has participated in the creation of our cities . . . God anticipated the development of your city. He marked off a place for it.' The surprising inference goes like this: 'When we acknowledge the placement of our cities as a function of God's sovereignty, we begin to see things we have never seen before.' Dawson believes that each city is where it is for God's purposes:

> Each city has a special redemptive gift for the world – a set of positive possibilities for righteousness and truth and the glory of God that Satan has taken, distorted, and used for evil. 'Satan is not a creator. He cannot originate anything. He can only turn created things and people to his own purposes.'

(Dawson, *Taking Our Cities for God*)

He then asks, 'What is your city's redemptive gift?'

Prayer pioneer and writer Alice Smith has insight here:

> The first consideration in discerning a city is to ask the Lord what the REDEMPTIVE GIFT of the city might be. A redemptive gift is a distinct characteristic about that city God can use to demonstrate his divine blessing and truth. What is true about the city in the natural will often be true in the Spirit.
>
> For instance, the first name given to Jerusalem was Salem. (See Genesis 14.18–20.) Salem means 'peace.' Jerusalem means 'habitation of peace.' God's redemptive plan is to see Jerusalem be a habitation of peace for all nations. Is it now? No. Will it be? Yes! In fact, all of Psalm 122 is dedicated to pray the truth about the city of Jerusalem. Until that time, Satan will focus on replacing the redemptive gift of the city with a destructive gift.
>
> How do you decide what might be the redemptive gift for your city? What are the most outstanding features of your city? What is your city known for?

- Hospitals?
- Waterways?
- Trade?
- Entertainment?
- The people?
- Manufacturing?

- Agriculture?
- Historical landmarks?
- Mountains?
- Climate?

(Smith, 'Redemptive Gift of Your City')

Cambridge is known for its world-leading university. Addenbrokes Hospital is a pioneer facility. The Cambridge Christian Union has helped lead the worldwide Church through the influence of those who served their spiritual apprenticeship there. The technological parks on the fringe of the city are innovators who help lead the way in international computing. This city has great influence, for good or for bad. What gift has your area for the wider community in your nation?

Just do it

A unique aspect of British church life at this time is the way that many are communicating to wide sections of the church about city-changing, life-enhancing and personal restoration projects. The Cinnamon Network helps share the core paperwork and best practice of many projects for the benefit of the UK church. Other projects such as Movement Day and GatherUK bring us together in structured conferences to discover the rich treasure that one group may have that would benefit others in the body of Christ.

City-Changing Prayer outlines how God called hundreds of churches together over a seven-year period to pray for Manchester. There are plenty of practical ideas contained in the book and lots to inspire you. It may sound obvious but if you want to see God move powerfully to transform your area, it really must begin with prayer; preferably prayer that draws together different expressions of church in a shared commitment to pray outwardly for the benefit of a town or city.

You could also do that on a smaller scale in your city. Work together so you can work better apart. Alice Smith notes:

There are unique churches in every city. What does your church body have that other churches in your city do not have? Is your

119

church exceptionally structured for missions? Do you know of some churches who have a powerful prayer ministry? Are some churches great at evangelism? How about those churches where they excel in their teaching and training methods?

Each is unique and is a redemptive gift of God to your city. Instead of criticizing the city church, learn to appreciate the diversity and contribution each brings to the whole.

(Smith, 'Redemptive Gift of Your City')

The hard stuff, the good stuff and the crown

Just recently I was invited to speak at the Labour Party Conference church service. I was told that Jeremy Corbyn (leader of the Labour Party) and a large number of MPs would be attending. The theme for the service was 'United we stand, divided we fall. Are we brave enough to work together?'

I suppose that this is the kind of invitation I would never have expected a few years ago. But it comes as a result of years of commitment to building partnerships. My Facebook and Twitter pages are attracting some interesting comments. People have such a lot of things to say when it comes to politics! This invitation says little or nothing about my political beliefs, but it is an interesting opportunity to speak about an important subject, unity of purpose.

Do we have to agree about everything in order to partner? I would say no.

I remember Andy Glover, the leader of Hoole Baptist Church, Chester, asking me this question a few years ago. Did they need every church in Chester to unite in order to see transformation? You certainly need some churches to work together, but don't wait for everyone to come on board as that's a sure way to prevent any action.

We cannot engage in community partnerships as believers together and with outside agencies without being aware of how many of our institutions in society have left behind their faith roots. How can we prevent compromise? How can we keep alive the spirituality that keeps us engaged in community transformation? Books can and have been written about this so what follows are just some thought starters.

- Shape our work around the witness of the local church in our communities. Churches last longer and cohere to their core values much longer than independent agencies.
- Place our spiritual values at the heart of our activity – such as the prayer emphasis of ROC.
- Have a Mars Hill attitude – Acts 17 tells us that Paul engaged in dialogue with those from other faiths. He noted that there was some common ground but many differences. We're not seeking to work together because 'all roads lead to God'. We're seeking common ground about specific issues. Paul was prepared to listen as well as talk.
- Listen to history. Christian campaigner Lord Shaftesbury worked with the Chartists, enlightened industrialists and many others to see the Factory Acts through Parliament and to ensure better lives for children and workers generally. Were these people natural allies? No. Wilberforce helped an unlikely coalition of Moravians, Wesleyans, Quakers, Anglicans, among others, to work together for the abolition of slavery.

Find the common ground and build on it. Some of our most un-likely partnerships have been the most fruitful. An obvious example is how we received The FUSE as an asset transfer because the Cabinet Office and Department for Education were impressed by our work. Partnerships are vital for transformation to be possible. It all starts and is maintained by prayer. The kingdom of God is expanding.

Over the past few years we have delivered over 165 community engagement events, ROC Conversations, around the UK. Each has an Action Group, made up of a variety of different agencies and led by a local church. These groups promote partnership working. It's a way of ensuring that partners work together. It's our way of helping churches to connect with other agencies for the greater good. We often say, 'If it's not a partnership, it's not ROC.'

We felt some time ago that we should be connecting these groups together across the UK to form a network. A regular newsletter goes out by email to the Action Group leaders. Effective communication is such a key component in community well-being. People often say to me, 'There is such a lot of good work going on but we didn't know about it.' These newsletters help share good ideas so that we can learn from one another and get better at what we do. We also share prayer needs.

Each ROC Conversation prays for the next one in the diary. Recently we held a Conversation in Canterbury, Kent. The next day they started to pray for the two we were holding in Northern Ireland. The minister of Canterbury Baptist Church, Andrew Fitzgerald, had family in Northern Ireland. He asked if he could join us on the trip. His prayers during our time over there were invaluable.

You can help people do together what they could not do apart. Think of your city and what you can do together. In Eastbourne, 27 churches work together (PARCHE) so that between them they can visit 67 of the 74 care homes. Their unity has bought them favour with the care home providers. Specific churches take responsibility for various care homes so that a weekly or monthly Christian service can take place there.

Dream a dream for where you live. You can be confident that God will go with you. Think on these words from Psalm 103, which capture much of the heart of what it means be a prayerful mountain-moving people.

> Praise the LORD, my soul,
> and forget not all his benefits –
> who forgives all your sins
> and heals all your diseases,
> who redeems your life from the pit
> and crowns you with love and compassion.
> (Psalm 103.2–4)

A crown speaks of authority. Our love and compassion will be our authority in the eyes of our communities.

May God use us to move more mountains in his name!

References and resources

Batterson, Mark (2012) *Draw the Circle: The 40-Day Prayer Challenge.* Grand Rapids, MI: Zondervan.

Claiborne, Shane, Wilson-Hartgrove, Jonathan, and Okoro, Enuma (2010) *Common Prayer: A Liturgy for Ordinary Radicals.* Grand Rapids, MI: Zondervan.

Dawson, John (2002, rev. edn) *Taking Our Cities for God.* Lake Mary, FL: Charisma House.

Department for Communities and Local Government (2009) *Improving Opportunity, Strengthening Society.* London: Department for Communities and Local Government.

Green, Debra and Frank (2005) *City-Changing Prayer.* Eastbourne: Kingsway Publications.

Greig, Pete (2007) *God on Mute: Engaging the Silence of Unanswered Prayer.* Eastbourne: Kingsway Publications.

Hamel, John, 'How and When to Pray the Prayer of Agreement'. Available online at: <www.johnhamelministries.org/SBP_4_Prayer_Agreement .htm>.

Hostetler, Bob (2016) 'Pray Like Job'. Available online at: <www.guideposts .org/faith-and-prayer/prayer-stories/pray-effectively/pray-like-job>.

Lewis, C. S. (1964) *Letters to Malcolm: Chiefly on Prayer.* New York: Harcourt, Brace & World.

Lupson, Peter (2006) *Thank God for Football.* London: SPCK.

Müller, George, with Parsons, Charles R. (2011) *An Hour with George Müller: The Man of Faith to Whom God Gave Millions.* Whitefish, MT: Literary Licensing.

Nappa, Mike (2014) 'Matthew 7:7–12; Ask, Seek, Knock'. Available online at: <www.beliefnet.com/columnists/forbiblestudynerds/2014/11/matthew -77-12-ask-seek-knock-theological-commentary.html>.

Ross, Lisa Brown (2015) '6 Powerful Lessons from the Book of Esther'. Available online at: <www.ibelieve.com/faith/6-powerful-life-lessons -from-the-book-of-esther.html>.

Smith, Alice (2009) 'Redemptive Gift of Your City'. Available online at: <http://nppnblog.blogspot.com/2009/08/your-citys-redemptive-gift.html>.

Thrasher, Bill (2009) *A Journey to Victorious Praying: Finding Discipline and Delight in Your Prayer Life.* Chicago, IL: Moody Press.

References and resources

Welby, Justin (2015) 'Prayer Is a Partnership with God'. Available online at: <www.archbishopofcanterbury.org/prayer-partnership-god>.

Willard, Dallas (2012) *Hearing God: Developing a Conversational Relationship with God*. Downers Grove, IL: InterVarsity Press.

Contact information

Redeeming Our Communities (ROC)
The FUSE
Warburton Lane
Partington
Manchester M31 4BU

Tel.: 0161 393 4511
Email: info@roc.uk.com
        chiefexecpa@roc.uk.com

https://roc.uk.com
https://roc.uk.com/shop
https://roc.uk.com/mmp
usethefuse.co.uk

Twitter: @debrajgreen; @weareROC
Instagram: debrajeangreen; wearerocuk
Facebook: www.facebook.com/wearerocuk/
            www.facebook.com/debra.green.1257

Wikipedia: https://en.wikipedia.org/wiki/Debra_Green

MOUNTAIN MOVING PRAYER

 ROC PRAYER COURSE

 101 COMMUNITY IDEAS

 DEBRA'S INTRODUCTION
VIDEO TO EACH CHAPTER

To access these essential extra
features, follow the link below.
https://roc.uk.com/mmp